WE

WO[...]

SEE

JESUS

Roy and Revel Hession

CHRISTIAN LITERATURE CRUSADE
Fort Washington, Pennsylvania 19034

CHRISTIAN LITERATURE CRUSADE
Fort Washington, Pennsylvania 19034

CANADA
Box 189, Elgin, Ontario KOG 1E0

GREAT BRITIAN
The Dean, Alresford, Hampshire

AUSTRALIA
P.O. Box 91, Pennant Hills, N.S.W. 2120

NEW ZEALAND
Box 1688, Auckland, C.1

Fourth printing 1961
Second edition 1961
Eighth printing 1972
Pocketbook edition 1973
Sixth printing 1978

SBN 87508-237-8

CONTENTS

PREFACE

THIS is a book that seeks to be simply about the Lord Jesus Christ Himself.

We Would See Jesus is somewhat of an amplification of *The Calvary Road* which was published in 1950 and which God has been pleased to bless to many in various parts of the world. We believe that this book will be found to carry on from where the other left off.

The first book dealt with various aspects of the Christian life and revival, such as brokenness, fulness, fellowship, and so on. It is, of course, helpful to have Christian experience dealt with aspect by aspect. We have since learned, however, that we do not need to itemise the Christian life; it is enough to see Jesus. Seeing Him we are convicted of sin, broken, cleansed, filled with the Spirit, set free from bondage, and revived. Each aspect of Christian experience is made real in us just by seeing Him. He is both the Blessing we all seek and the easily accessible Way to that blessing. If we concentrate on trying to make a certain aspect of things "work", it will become a formula for us and will only lead us into bondage. But the Lord Jesus has come to take from us every yoke of bondage and to set us free to serve Him in the freshness and spontaneity of the Spirit, and all that by the simple sight of Him which the Holy Spirit gives to the eye of faith.

> We would see Jesus, this is all we're needing;
> Strength, joy, and willingness come with the sight;
> We would see Jesus, dying, risen, pleading;
> Then welcome day, and farewell mortal night.

This, then, is the direction and theme of the present book—Jesus. However, we cannot pretend that it is a complete treatment of such a theme. The reader will find much that has not been touched upon. But, as we have said, it is enough to see Jesus and to go on seeing Him. As we do so, we shall see everything else we need to see, as we need to see it, and all in its right relation to Him, who must ever be for us the centre.

Two words occur again and again in the following pages, and they are used in a special sense. As we have not thought it right to interrupt the flow of thought with chapters to amplify their meaning, we think it well to insert something here as to the sense in which these words are used.

The first is the word "grace". So often people speak of this as some blessing which we receive from God at special times. We have, however, sought to use it in the strictly New Testament sense of the word. There, it is the great word of our salvation and of all God's dealings with us; for it is written, "By grace are ye saved through faith." Nothing is more important than that we should apprehend its meaning in both our minds and experience. Missing this, we miss everything. In the New Testament grace is not a blessing or an influence from God which we receive, but rather an attribute of God which governs His attitude to man, and can be defined as the undeserved love and favour of God. Romans 11 : 6 says, "And if by grace, then is it no more of works; otherwise grace is no more grace." The whole essence of grace is that it is undeserved. The moment we have to do something to make ourselves more acceptable to God, or the moment we have to have a certain feeling or attribute of character in order to be blessed of God, then grace is no more grace. Grace permits us to come (nay, demands that we come) as empty sinners to be blessed, empty of right feelings, good character, and satisfactory record, with nothing to commend ourselves but our deep need, fully and frankly acknowledged. Then grace, being what it is, is drawn by that need to satisfy it, just as water is drawn to depth that it might fill it. This means that when at last we are content to find no merit nor procuring cause in ourselves, and are willing to admit the full extent of our sinfulness, then there is no limit to what God will do for the poor who look to Him in their nothingness. If what we receive from God is dependent, even to a small extent, on what we are or do, then the most we can expect is but an intermittent trickle of blessing. But if what we are to receive is to be measured by the grace of God quite apart from works, then there is only one word that adequately describes what He pours upon us, the word which so often is linked with grace in the New Testament, "abundance"! The struggle, of course, is to believe it and to be willing to be but empty sinners to the end of our days, that grace may continue to match our needs.

> When we come to the end of our hoarded resources,
> Our Father's full giving has only begun.
> His love has no limit, His grace has no measure,
> His power no boundary known unto men;
> For out of His infinite riches in Jesus
> He giveth, and giveth, and giveth again.

This, then, is grace and this is God! What a melting vision this gives us of Him!

The other word that needs a little explanation as to its use in these pages is the word "revival". The popular sense in which this word is used is that of a general and more or less spectacular movement of the Holy Spirit, in which many are saved and the Church built up. That this is a legitimate use of the word we would not deny, but we have used it throughout in the sense of the work of God which He does firstly in the lives of believers, and which is both personal and immediate for each believer who recognises the decline there has been in his Christian experience, who bows to the dealings of God with him, and who sees Jesus as all he needs and believingly apprehends Him as such. It is simply this that lies at the heart of even the most spectacular movements of revival. After all, what are such movements but the communication of this life to ever-increasing numbers? And what does God use to this end but the radiant testimonies of the revived themselves? It is plain, then, that our first responsibility is to be revived ourselves, and to give our testimony to those around us. We can trust God, then, to fit us and the life He is giving us into whatever corporate movement of His Spirit that He pleases.

May God grant that every reader have an abundant fulfilment of the longing, expressed long ago by the Greeks to Philip, "Sir, we would see Jesus" (John 12 : 21).

Roy and Revel Hession

CHAPTER I

SEEING GOD—THE PURPOSE OF LIFE

My goal is God Himself, not joy, nor peace,
Nor even blessing, but Himself, my God.

WHAT is the purpose of life? This is the one question to which most of us are longing to find the answer. We find ourselves driven and pulled in different directions by inner urges, longings, and desires which we do not seem able to satisfy. We look enviously at others and imagine that their lives are much fuller and more satisfying than ours. We think that if we could gain this prize or enjoy that pleasure, we should be truly satisfied; but when at last we do achieve those prizes or pleasures we find that we are no happier than we were before. And the older we grow, the more frustrated we feel, and we find ourselves asking, "What is the purpose of life? How can I find it? How can I be sure it is the right one?" These are questions to which many a professing Christian yet needs to find the answer, as well as the man who has no knowledge of God.

However, when we turn to the Bible we find a clear and simple answer to this fundamental question. It plainly states that there is but one purpose for mankind, and that purpose is the same, whatever our sex, our age, our nationality, or status in society.

"What doth the Lord thy God require of thee, but to fear the Lord thy God, to walk in all His ways, and to love Him" (Deut. 10 : 12).

"He hath showed thee, O man, what is good; and what doth the Lord require of thee, but to . . . humble thyself to walk with thy God" (Mic. 6 : 8 (margin)).

"Thou shalt love the Lord thy God with all thy heart, and with all thy soul, and with all thy mind, and with all thy strength" (Mark 12 : 30).

It appears, therefore, that the Bible answer to the question,

9

"What is the purpose of life?" is to know, and to love, and to walk with God; that is, to see God. Indeed, men in former times came to speak of "the end of life" as being the "Vision of God". The divines who in the seventeenth century produced the Westminster Confession answered the question, "What is the chief end of man?" with the words, "Man's chief end is to glorify God, and to enjoy Him for ever."

Today, however, we do not hear much about the need to see God. It is only as we turn the pages of the past that we become aware of our lack of this emphasis, both in preaching and in living the Gospel. In former days, we find, even in times of spiritual darkness, that there were always some who were gripped by a consuming passion—the longing to see God. For them there was only one goal, to know their God. They were heart-thirsty, and they knew that God alone could satisfy their thirst. As we read of their search for God, we find some travelling along strange paths. We see them living in desert or cave, or withdrawing to the monastery. In their desire for that holiness "without which no man shall see the Lord" (Heb. 12 : 14), they might strip themselves of every earthly possession, or mortify their bodies by self-inflicted torture. They were sometimes fanatical, sometimes morbidly introspective. We look back on many of them now as poor, misguided souls who were in bondage to legalism and asceticism. But let us always remember that these things were done in the longing and search for God, and that their emphasis was on personal holiness in order to see God.

At the present time the situation is very different. We have much more light on the Bible and the message of the Gospel, and we look back rather despisingly on many of these seekers of old. But the solemnising fact is this, that the coming of more light has not brought an increasing passion to see God. In fact, it seems to have had the reverse effect. That deep hunger for God Himself is patently lacking, and it would appear that we have lowered our goal in the Christian life to something less than God Himself.

Two emphases stand out today.

First of all, instead of stressing holiness in order to *see* God, the emphasis is on service *for* God. We have come to think of the Christian life as consisting in serving God as fully and as efficiently as we can. Techniques and methods, by which we hope to make God's message known, have become the important thing. To carry out this service we need power, and so instead of a longing for God, our longing is for power to serve Him more effectively. So much has service become the centre of our thinking that very often a man's rightness with God is judged by his success or otherwise in his Christian work.

2 Then there tends to be today an emphasis on the seeking of inner spiritual experiences. While so many Christians are content to live at a very low level, it is good that some do become concerned about their Christian lives, and it is right that they should. However, the concern arises not so much from a hunger for God, but from a longing to find an inner experience of happiness, joy, and power, and we find ourselves looking for "it", rather than God Himself.

Both these ends fall utterly short of the great end that God has designed for man, that of glorifying Him and enjoying Him for ever. They fail to satisfy God's heart and they fail to satisfy ours.

*   *   *   *   *

To understand why the seeing of God should be the main goal of life and why He should make such a claim on us, we must turn our minds back to the very dawn of history.

The story of man began when God, who is complete in Himself and therefore could have no needs, deliberately chose, it would seem, to be incomplete without creatures of His own creating. "Thou hast created all things, and *for Thy pleasure* they are and were created" (Rev. 4:11). It was for this purpose and no other, that of existing for the pleasure of God, that man was brought into being. He was intended to be the delight of God and the object of His affection. On man's side, the basis of that original relationship was that it was completely God-centred. Man knew that he had only been created to delight God, and his only concern was to respond to the Divine affection, to live for Him, and to do His will. It was his joy

Memorize!

continually to submit his will and desires to those of his Creator, and in nothing to be independent of Him. As he thus lived in submission to God, every need in man's nature was satisfied by God. As C. S. Lewis puts it in describing that early unfallen relationship, "In perfect cyclic movement, being, power and joy descended from God to man in the form of gift and returned from man to God in the form of obedient love and ecstatic adoration." Truly these were the "palmy days" of the human race, when man was as much at home in the unseen realm as in the seen, when the faculty within him called spirit was able to commune with God who is Spirit.

To insist, then, that to see God and be in living relationship with Him is the supreme goal of life is not to insist on anything strange or unnatural. It is the very purpose for which we were created, the sole *raison d'être* for our being on the earth at all.

More than that, however, for us to see God is the sole purpose of God's redemption of the world by the Lord Jesus Christ; for man soon lost the Divine purpose for his life, and needed to be redeemed. That loving, submissive relationship with God did not last long. Those walks together in the cool of the day came to an end, for one day sin stalked into the garden. Under the temptation of Satan, who suggested that by a simple act of transgression man could forsake the creaturely position and become "as gods" (Gen. 3 : 5), man deliberately chose no longer to be dependent on God. He set himself up on his own, putting himself at the centre of his world, where before he had delighted to put God. Thereafter he became a proud, unbroken spirit. No longer would he willingly submit to his Creator; no longer would he recognise that he was made for God. Moreover, on God's side the foundation of His fellowship with man was destroyed, because God in His holiness could not have fellowship with man who was unholy. There could never be fellowship between light and darkness, between holiness and sin; and man instinctively realised this, for his first reaction was to hide from the presence of the Lord God behind the trees of the garden.

We, too, descendants of those first sinners, are involved in all this. We are born with the same God-defiant nature that

Adam acquired the day he first sinned. We all start life as "I" specialists, as someone has quaintly put it, and our actions are governed by self-interest. Such is the rebellious attitude of man to God's authority now that the Bible is driven to say "There is none that understandeth, there is none that seeketh after God" (Rom. 3 : 11). The natural heart defies God and says, "Depart from us; for we desire not the knowledge of Thy ways. What is the Almighty, that we should serve Him?" (Job 21 : 14, 15).

Thus did man lose the original Divine purpose of his life. Had God chosen to leave man there, in his alienation and in all the miseries that would inevitably follow, no angel in the sky could have charged Him with injustice, nor even with lack of love. He had already showered upon man His love, and man had thrown that love back in His face. But the love of God was such that, when man had done all that, He yet purposed his recovery, and He stretched out His hand the second time, this time to redeem. To create, God had but to speak, and it was done. But to redeem, He had to bleed. And He did so in the Person of His Son, Jesus Christ, whom He sent to take for us the place of death upon the Cross which our sin had so richly deserved. Redemption, however, was no last-minute thought, brought into being to meet an unexpected emergency. No sooner had sin entered the garden than God spoke of One who was to come and who was to bruise the serpent's (that is, Satan's) head, His own heel being bruised in the process (Gen. 3 : 15), and to restore all the damage which sin and Satan had done. God thereby revealed that the sad turn of events had not taken Him by surprise, but that there was One in reserve to meet this very situation. Scripture calls Him "the Lamb slain from the foundation of the world" (Rev. 13 : 8), because with God the remedy antedated the disease. And all this was done with the one purpose of bringing us fallen men with our sinful, proud, unbroken natures back to that relationship with God of submissiveness and God-centredness that was lost in the Fall, and where once more He can delight in us and we in Him.

If to bring us back into this relationship with God is the whole purpose of His creation and then His redemption of us, we can be quite sure that this will be the one great object of all His present dealings with us. If an aeroplane designer designs a plane to fly at a certain altitude and finds that it will not leave the ground, he will bend every effort to make that plane do that for which he designed it. So does God bend every effort to bring us back to Himself. An initial repentance on our part and our conversion to God is only the gateway to the road back to fellowship with Himself. It is only when we get on the road that God can start dealing with our self-centred wills, so that, painful though it is to wills "swollen and inflamed by years of usurpation", we come back to the place of submission and God-centredness. If we will not from our own choice seek Him and want Him, He often has to allow sorrow, suffering, trials, ill-health, smashed plans, and failure, so that in our need we will find our need of Him. Such suffering, however, is never punitive, but wholly and only restorative in its intention. It is Love humbling us and drawing us to the place of repentance and to God.

*   *   *   *   *

In the light of all this, we can see how far short the goals we set ourselves, such as service and activity for God and the finding of special inner experiences, fall from the great goal God has purposed for us.

To concentrate on service and activity for God may often actively thwart our attaining of the true goal, God Himself. At first sight it seems heroic to fling our lives away in the service of God and of our fellows. We feel it is bound to mean more to Him than our experience of Him. Service seems so unselfish, whereas concentrating on our walk with God seems selfish and self-centred. But it is the very reverse. The things that God is most concerned about are our coldness of heart towards Himself and our proud, unbroken natures. Christian service of itself can, and so often does, leave our self-centred nature untouched. That is why there is scarcely a church, a mission station, or a committee undertaking a special piece of service, that is without an unresolved problem of personal relationships eating out its heart and thwarting its progress.

This is because Christian service often gives us opportunities of leadership and position that we could not attain in the secular world, and we quickly fall into pride, self-seeking, and ambition. With those things hidden in our hearts, we have only to work alongside others, and we find resentment, hardness, criticism, jealousy, and frustration issuing from our hearts. We think we are working for God, but the test of how little of our service is for Him is revealed by our resentment or self-pity, when the actions of others, or circumstances, or ill-health take it from us!

In this condition we are trying to give to others an answer which we have not truly and deeply found for ourselves. The tragedy is that much of the vast network of Christian activity and service is bent on propagating an answer for people's needs and problems which few of those propagating it are finding adequate in their own lives. We need to leave our lusting for ever-larger spheres of Christian service and concentrate on seeing God for ourselves and finding the deep answer for life in Him. Then, even if we are located in the most obscure corner of the globe, the world will make a road to our door to get that answer. Our service of help to our fellows then becomes incidental to our vision of God, and the direct consequence of it.

This does not mean that God does not want us engaged actively in His service. He does; but His purpose is often far different from what we think. Our service, in His mind, is to be far more the potter's wheel on which He can mould us than the achieving of those spectacular objectives on which we set our hearts. He sees a sharp point in our make-up that is continually wounding others. He sees within our hearts the motives of self-seeking and pride. He, therefore, allows someone to come and work alongside us who will rub against that sharp point and round it off. Or He allows someone to thwart our plans and to step into our shoes. If we are making service for Him an end in itself we will be full of reactions and will want to fight back or to break away and start an independent work of our own, and we become more self-centred than ever. But if we will bow to what God has allowed, and repent of our sinful reactions, we will find that that very situation has led us into a deeper experience of His grace and of His power to satisfy our hearts with Himself alone.

In the same way, the inordinate seeking of inner spiritual experiences may also thwart us finding our true goal, for if we make our purpose in life a quest for these things we tend to become occupied with our personal experiences or lack of them. This produces the sad situation of hungry, dissatisfied Christians seeking out this speaker or that, hoping that he will be found to have the secret; or going to this Convention or that Conference, trying new formulas for blessing, seeking fresh experiences, and falling either into pride or despair, according to whether they feel they have the blessing or not. This leaves the Christian still self-centred, occupied with himself and his experiences, and it can lead to much mental anguish through the confusion of our many teachings and emphases on sanctification and kindred doctrines. Yet, all the time the One who alone can satisfy the heart is by our side, longing to be known and loved and proved.

* * * * *

This, then, is the purpose of life, to see God, and to allow Him to bring us back to the old relationship of submission to Himself. We might wish that God would be content with some lesser purpose for us. As C. S. Lewis says, "It is natural to wish that God had designed for us a less glorious and arduous destiny. . . . It is a burden of glory, not only beyond our deserts, but also, except in rare moments of grace, beyond our desiring." * But we must not rebel against this high purpose for us. Clay does not argue with the potter. It knows that the potter has every right to make it into whatever shape He chooses. Our highest good is achieved only in submitting. It has been said that there is a God-shaped blank in every man's heart. It is also true that there is a man-shaped blank in God's heart. It is because of the latter that God yearns so much for us and pursues us so relentlessly, and it is because of the former that mere earthly things, even service, will never satisfy our hearts. Only God Himself can fill that blank which is made

* C. S. Lewis in *The Problem of Pain*.

Clay doesn't argue w/ the Potter. It submits

in His shape. If we will yield to this, some of us will have a new outlook on life. We will have a new zest for life, even in the dreariest surroundings. As soon as the emphasis is changed from "doing" to "being", there is an easing of tension. The situations may not change, but we have changed. If fellowship with God is to be our first concern, then we can have fellowship with God in the kitchen, in sickness, in any kind of trying and difficult situation. Whatever lies across our path to be done, even the most irksome chores, are there to be done for God and for His glory. Gone will be the former striving, bondage, and frustration. We shall be at peace with our God and ourselves.

> One thing I know, I cannot say Him nay;
> One thing I do, I press toward my Lord:
> My God my glory here from day to day,
> And in the glory there my great reward.

Emphasis change from "doing" to "being"

CHAPTER II

SEEING GOD IN THE FACE OF JESUS CHRIST

PERHAPS the previous chapter has left us feeling frustrated. We agree with the argument, we realise that our goal should be God Himself, but He seems far off, unknowable.

The fact is, God is unknowable, unless there is an easily appreciated revelation of Himself. Apart from that revelation, men have groped for Him in vain and have had to say with Job, "Oh, that I knew where I might find Him!" (Job. 23 : 3). Even the wonders of creation fail to give the revelation of Him that is needed. Of them, Job said, "Lo, these are but the out-skirts of His ways, and how small a whisper do we hear of Him" (Job 26 : 14 R.V.). Left to themselves, men arrive at a false knowledge of God, a knowledge that only begets fear and bondage, and which repels men rather than draws them to Him.

However, the glorious, central fact of Christianity is that God has made a full and final revelation of Himself which has made Him understandable, accessible, and desirable to the simplest and most fearful of us. He has done so in a Son, through whom He made the worlds and who, having humbled Himself to take on Him our flesh and blood, and by Himself to purge our sins, has sat down on the right hand of the Majesty on high. And that Son is the Lord Jesus.

The disciples themselves had battled with this difficulty of the unknowableness of God, and one day one of them said to the Lord Jesus, "Lord, show us the Father, and it sufficeth us." In reply, Jesus uttered the stupendous words, "He that hath seen Me hath seen the Father." (John 14 : 9). Later in the New Testament we find Paul saying the same thing to the Colossians, "His dear Son . . . who is the image of the invisible God." (Col. 1 : 15). And again, to the Corinthians, "God . . . hath shined in our hearts, to give the light of the knowledge of the glory of God in the face of Jesus Christ" (2 Cor. 4 : 6).

It is this verse about the light of the knowledge of the glory of God being seen in the face of Jesus Christ that helps us most here. Light is invisible unless it shines upon some object. We think we see a ray of sunshine shining into the room. But that is not so. We see only the particles in the air upon which the light shines and which thus reveal the presence of light. "God is light" (1 John 1 : 5) we read, but He is invisible and unknowable unless He shines upon some object that will reveal Him. The object upon which He has shone is the face of Jesus Christ, and as we look into that face, there shines in our hearts the light of the knowledge of the glory of God, which we can see nowhere else.

In yet other verses the New Testament gives us three beautiful illustrations of the way in which the Lord Jesus is the revelation of the Father. In one place He is called "the Word" (John 1 : 1), for the word is the expression of the thought. In another He is called "the express image of His Person" (Heb. 1 : 3), for the wax impress is the exact expression of the seal. And in the same verse He is called "the brightness of His glory", for the brightness of the rays express the sun, and are all that we can see of the sun. Yes, just as the word is the son of the thought, and the wax-impress the son of the seal, and the rays the son of the sun, so Jesus is the Son of God, equal to Him but never independent of Him and perfectly expressing Him to us in terms that we can simply appreciate. And He was all this, not merely at the Incarnation, but before time began, and will ever be so when time has ceased to be.

> Thou art the Everlasting Word,
>   The Father's only Son,
> God manifestly seen and heard
>   And heaven's beloved One.
>
> In Thee most perfectly expressed
>   The Father's glories shine;
> Of the full Deity possessed,
>   Eternally Divine.
>
> True image of the Infinite,
>   Whose essence is concealed;
> Brightness of uncreated light,
>   The heart of God revealed.

Nowhere else can we fully see God but in the face of Jesus
Christ.

In his biography of Martin Luther, D'Aubigné describes
how Luther was seeking to know God. He says that "he would
have wished to penetrate into the secret councils of God, to
unveil His mysteries, to see the invisible and to comprehend
the incomprehensible". Stupitz checked him. He told him not
to presume to fathom the hidden God, but to confine himself
to what He has manifested to us in Jesus Christ. In Him, God
has said, you will find what I am and what I require. Nowhere
else, neither in heaven nor in the earth, will you discover it.

*   *   *   *   *

What exactly is it that we see when we look into the face of
Jesus Christ? The verse we are considering says we see not
only "the light of the knowledge of God", but also the "light of
the knowledge of the *glory* of God in the face of Jesus Christ".
In Him we see not only God but His glory displayed. This gives
us a new understanding of that which makes God glorious—
and it comes as both a surprise and a shock. For the face that
reveals the glory of God is a marred face, spat upon and dis-
figured by the malice of men. The prophetic word of Isaiah
concerning Him, "His visage was so marred more than any
man, and His form more than the sons of men" (Isa. 52 : 14)
can really be translated "His visage was marred so that it was
no longer that of a man", so great was His disfigurement. But,
you say, that is not the vision of glory, but of shame and disgrace! However, it is glory as God counts glory, for the glory
of God consists in something other than what we suppose.
We are always falling into the mistake of thinking God is "such
an one as ourselves" (Psa. 50 : 21) and therefore that His glory
consists in much the same things as that in which man's glory
consists, only on a bigger scale. Man's glory is normally
thought to lie in his ability to exalt himself, and humble others
to his will. That is glory, that is power, says the world. "Men
will praise thee when thou doest well to thyself" (Psa. 49 : 18).
How often have we coveted the glory of being able to sit at a
desk as a high administrative chief and at the touch of a button

command men to do what we want! Glory in man's eyes is always that which exalts him.

In Jesus, however, we see that God's glory consists in the very reverse—not so much in His ability to exalt Himself and humble man, but in His willingness to humble Himself for the sake of man—not so much in a mighty display of power that would break in pieces those that oppose Him, but rather in the hiding of that power and the showing of grace to the undeserving when they turn to Him in repentance. When Moses said, "I beseech Thee, shew me Thy glory", God replied, "I will make all My goodness pass before thee" (Exod. 33 : 18, 19). Not, "I will make all My power, My majesty, My holiness pass before thee" but "I will make all My *goodness* to the weak, the sinful, and the undeserving pass before thee." In showing His goodness (grace, as it is called in the New Testament) He was showing His glory. His glory is His grace (Eph. 1 : 6). It is this that makes the angels hide their faces and bow in wondering adoration of God. And it is this glory which is fully seen in the face of Jesus and nowhere else. "In Him most perfectly expressed the Father's glories shine."

This was the conception of glory that occupied the Saviour's mind. On one occasion He said, "The hour is come that the Son of Man should be glorified" (John 12 : 23). A few verses farther on He speaks of it as an hour when He would be lifted up and would draw all men to Him (John 12 : 32). Again and again He had said, "Mine hour is not yet come." Now He says, "It is come." Were we reading all this for the first time, we would surely feel like saying at this point, "Never was the hour of glory and vindication more merited than in His case, for none had walked the path of vilification and opposition more patiently than He!" What is our surprise, then, when we discover that He is speaking, not of being lifted up on a Throne, but on a Tree, as a public spectacle of shame, and all that for rebellious man, that He might save him from the miseries of his sin. "This," says Jesus in effect, "is the hour of My glory, for it is the hour of My grace to sinners." In Jesus, then, we see that God's highest glory consists in His securing our deepest happiness. What a God is this!

How different is this sight of Him from the conception our guilty consciences have given us! A guilty conscience always makes us want to hide from Him, as if He were the God with the big stick! Little wonder, then, that He goes on to say, "I, if I be lifted up from the earth, [revealing the glory of God in grace] will draw all men unto Me." Here is a revelation of God that makes Him not only understandable but also infinitely desirable.

We need to look, then, no farther than the face of Jesus Christ to see God, and to know Him as He really is.

> In Him I see the Godhead shine,
> Christ for me!

How good of God to simplify our quest like this! We need not be philosophers, nor theologians, nor scholars. We need not—nay, we should not—pry any farther. All we need to know of the Father has been revealed in the Lord Jesus with such simplicity that a child can understand . . . perhaps with such simplicity that unless we become as little children we will not understand, for so often it is our intellect that gets in the way.

The one cry that we all need to utter is that of the Greeks to Philip, "Sir, we would see Jesus!" for, seeing Him, we see all, and every need of our hearts is met.

*   *   *   *   *

We must now ask ourselves what it actually means to "see Jesus". Perhaps it will help us to see what it does not mean.

To see Jesus does not mean that we are to seek to see Him in a mystical way, nor to crave for visions. We once heard someone, on being asked if they were seeing Jesus for themselves, reply, "Oh, yes, I am always trying to conjure up pictures of Him in my mind." Some people are given to visions, but visions are not to be sought after, nor gloried in. Paul was very reticent about what he had seen (2 Cor. 12 : 1–5). The fact of having a vision does not necessarily mean that we know the Lord Jesus more deeply than anyone else—sometimes it can be a hindrance.

Furthermore, we must not imagine that a merely objective contemplation of Christ and His love, or an academic delight in truth, is what is needed. Important as Bible study is, it can be strangely sterile and does not necessarily mean that the student is enjoying a transforming vision of the Lord Jesus Himself—though we shall never get very far without a patient and daily waiting on God over the Scriptures.

To see Jesus is to apprehend Him *as the supply of our present needs*, and believingly to lay hold on Him as such. The Lord Jesus is always seen through the eye of need. He is presented to us in the Scriptures not for our academic contemplation and delight, but for our desperate need as sinners and weaklings. The acknowledgment of need and the confession of sin, therefore, is ever the first step in seeing Jesus. Then, where there is acknowledged need, the Holy Spirit delights to show to the heart the Lord Jesus as the supply of just that need. Basically He is revealed through the Scriptures, but often in other ways too—through another's testimony, through the words of a hymn, or through the even more direct approach of the Spirit to the soul without any such means. Then, as the soul believingly appropriates for himself what the Spirit shows of Jesus, striving, strain, a consciousness of guilt, fear, and sorrow flee away and "our mouth is filled with laughter and our tongue with singing "(Psa. 126 : 2).

CHAPTER III

SEEING JESUS AS ALL WE NEED

O NE of the most breathtaking occasions when Jesus claimed equality with the Father was when He said, "Before Abraham was, I am" (John 8 : 58). The sentence immediately challenges our attention because of the extraordinary liberty it takes with our grammar. If the Lord Jesus had merely wanted to express His pre-existence, He would surely have said, "Before Abraham was, I was." But He says, "Before Abraham was, I AM."

Without any doubt He is taking us back to that day when Moses, bowing before God at the burning bush, asked what name he should give the God who was sending him to the Children of Israel. God's reply then was, "I AM THAT I AM. Thus shalt thou say unto the Children of Israel, I AM hath sent me unto you . . . Jehovah, God of your fathers, hath sent me unto you: this is My name for ever, and this is My memorial unto all generations" (Exod. 3 : 14, 15). Thereafter, God's personal name became Jehovah, which comes from the same Hebrew root as I AM, and means the same.

Thus it was, when the Lord Jesus said this word to the Jews, He dared to claim to be the great I AM of the Old Testament, whom they all knew to be the covenant God of their fathers. He went farther, saying that for them their own eternal destiny would depend on their accepting Him as such, for, said He, "If ye believe not that I AM, ye shall die in your sins" (John 8 : 24).*

The meaning of this great name, Jehovah, that is, I AM, which Jesus claimed for Himself is twofold. It means first of all that He is the Ever-present One, who stands outside of

* The word "He" is in italics in the Authorised (King James) Version, which means it is not in the Greek and can be omitted. This throws into relief the name, "I am".

time, to whom there is no past nor future, but to whom everything is present. Clearly, that is the first meaning of this strange mixture of tenses . . . "Before Abraham was, I AM." And that surely is what eternity is—not merely elongated time, but another realm altogether where everything is one glorious present. It is for this reason that the French Bible always translates the name, Jehovah, as "L'Éternel", the Eternal One.

The relation of the Eternal One to us in time can be illustrated by the relation of a reader to the events in a book. In the story in the book there is a sequence of time. As the pages are turned, certain incidents go into the past, others come into the present and yet others remain in the future. And yet the reader himself is in another realm altogether. He can open the book at any page, and to him the incidents there are all present, actually happening at that moment, as he reads them. What a vision this gives of our Lord Jesus, the Eternal One, the I AM! To Him our lives with their past and future are all present; our yesterdays as well as our tomorrows are all *now* to Him.

More important for us, however, is the fact that this name, Jehovah, is used almost uniformly in connection with that earthly people to whom He brought Himself into covenant obligations, the Children of Israel. To the Gentile nations, He was just God. But to His chosen people, to whom He had pledged special promises, He was ever Jehovah.* The fact that this Name was intended to have a special significance to them is made clear when God says to Moses, "I am Jehovah: and I appeared unto Abraham, unto Isaac, and unto Jacob, by the name of God Almighty, but by My name Jehovah was I not known to them" (Exod. 6 : 2, 3). Quite obviously, then, this name is meant to convey to them a new and precious revelation. What is it?

---

* The pity is that the Authorised Version largely obscures the use of the name "Jehovah" by almost always using the word "Lord" in the translation—doubtless carried over from the Jewish tradition that the name of Jehovah was too sacred to write. The version, however, does help us by putting "LORD" all in capitals, whenever it is Jehovah in the original. The same applies whenever "God" is spelled with capital letters, GOD. Watch for it.

The special revelation which this name gives is that of the grace of God. "I am" is an unfinished sentence. It has no object. I am—what? What is our wonder when we discover, as we continue with our Bibles, that He is saying, "I AM whatever My people need" and that the sentence is only left blank that man may bring his many and various needs, as they arise, to complete it!

Apart from human need this great name of God goes round and round in a closed circle, "I am that I am"—which means that God is incomprehensible. But the moment human need and misery present themselves, He becomes just what that person needs. The verb has at last an object, the sentence is complete and God is revealed and known. Do we lack peace? "I am thy peace," He says. Do we lack strength? "I am thy strength." Do we lack spiritual life? "I am thy life." Do we lack wisdom? "I am thy wisdom", and so on.

The name "Jehovah" is really like a blank cheque. Your faith can fill in what He is to be to you—just what you need, as each need arises. It is not you, moreover, who are beseeching Him for this privilege, but He who is pressing it upon you. He is asking you to ask. "Hitherto have ye asked nothing in My name: ask, and ye shall receive, that your joy may be full" (John 16 : 24). Just as water is ever seeking the lowest depths in order to fill them, so is Jehovah ever seeking out man's need in order to satisfy it. Where there is need, there is God. Where there is sorrow, misery, unhappiness, suffering, confusion, folly, oppression, there is the I AM, yearning to turn man's sorrow into bliss whenever man will let Him. It is not, therefore, the hungry seeking for bread, but the Bread seeking the hungry; not the sad seeking for joy, but rather Joy seeking the sad; not emptiness seeking fulness, but rather Fulness seeking emptiness. And it is not merely that He supplies our need, but He becomes Himself the fulfilment of our need. He is ever "I am that which My people need".

Oh, the grace of it, the surprise of it! Why should He? What claim have we on Him for this? Even man before the Fall had no claim on his God for this, much less man who has rebelled and fallen, and most of whose needs and miseries are but the result of his own sin! But that is grace and that is God. Grace, being what it is, is always drawn by need. And this is no extra nor afterthought on the part of God. It is His way of revealing Himself. Apart from our need, He is "I am that I am", but as He is allowed to become the fulfilment of our need, He is seen for what He really is. That is why a mere academic understanding of the things of God is never the way to see Him and to know Him. It is as we come to Him with our needs that then "thou shalt know that I am the Jehovah".

Sometimes in the Old Testament this blank cheque, the name "Jehovah", is filled in for us, to encourage us to fill it in ourselves, as we have need. Every now and then we come across Jehovah compounded with another word to form His completed name for that occasion. In one place the Children of Israel had need of a banner to rally their drooping spirits and to lead them into victory against the forces that lay against them as they journeyed through the wilderness. They found their Jehovah God to be just that to them, and so, after the victory over Amalek, they built an altar and called the name of it Jehovah–Nissi, which means "I am thy banner" (Exod. 17 : 15). It was His warfare, not merely theirs.

In another place Gideon feared for his life, for he had seen an angel of Jehovah face to face. Then Jehovah said to him, "Peace be unto thee; fear not: thou shalt not die." Thus it was discovered that Jehovah was peace, even to a sinner like Gideon, and to commemorate the new revelation he built an altar unto Jehovah and called it "Jehovah-Shalom", meaning "I am thy peace" (Judges 6 : 24).

In yet another place Jeremiah says of the Messiah who was to come, "In His days Judah shall be saved, and Israel shall dwell safely: and this is His name whereby He shall be called, 'Jehovah–Tsidkenu'", that is, "I am thy righteousness" (Jer. 23 : 6 (margin)). Israel shall be saved and dwell safely because Jehovah will stand for them, answering every accusation against them, becoming their surety and righteousness.

So it goes on, seven such wonderful compounds of Jehovah,*

* The remaining four are: Genesis 22 : 14 (Jehovah-Jireh, I am the One who provides); Exodus 15 : 26 (Jehovah-Rapha, I am the One who

seven places in the Old Testament, where the cheque "I am" is filled up for us for our encouragement. What a study these compound names are! That, however, is outside the scope of this little book, for our aim is to fix our attention on the supreme compound of Jehovah—JESUS. This might be written JE-SUS, and, it seems, is but a contraction of Jehovah-Sus,* which simply means, "I am thy Salvation". Sooner or later, if Jehovah means, "I am what you need", He will have to undertake our basic need as sinners. As such, we are justly condemned by His holy law, and we languish in the misery and famine of the "far country" of our own choosing. All the other needs which the other compound names of Jehovah reveal Him as meeting are not especially the needs of His people as sinners. But in Jesus, Jehovah undertakes to be what His people need *as sinners*, without excuse and without rights.

God could have undertaken His people's other needs without sending Jesus. He did so in the Old Testament, and He could have continued to do so in our time. But when it came to His people's needs *as sinners*—it had to be Jesus. There was no other way. There was no other good enough to pay the price of sin. And God did not withhold Him. He so loved us that He sent Him, the brightness of His glory and the express image of His person, to effect by the shedding of His blood a full redemption from sin for us, and as a risen Saviour to be continuously all His people need, as sinners—for our need as sinners is continuous, right up to the gates of heaven.

We can now say, not only where there is *need*, there is God,

---

heals); Psalms 23 : 1 (Jehovah-Ra-ah, I am thy shepherd); Ezekiel 48 : 35 (Jehovah-Shammah, I am the One who is there, or, who is present). In some cases the Authorised Version does not give the Hebrew name, but merely the English translation of it.

* Actually, the name "Jesus" is the Greek form of the Hebrew name "Jehoshua". The first letters of this name "Je" are a contraction of "Jehovah", and are linked with a Hebrew name meaning "salvation" to make the full name, "Jehovah is salvation". Joshua is a further contraction of Jehoshua. Therefore Jehoshua, Joshua, and Jesus are all the same name, the first two being the Hebrew forms, and the last one the Greek form. This explains why Joshua is called Jesus in Hebrews 4 : 8.

but where there is *sin*, there is Jesus—and that is something far more wonderful. There is not always something blameworthy in a need, and we can understand God being touched and drawn by humanity's need. But humanity's sin, surely that does not draw Him, except in judgment. But no—just because God is what He is, and Jesus is what He is, and grace is what it is, it is gloriously true, where there is sin, there is always Jesus—seeking to forgive sin and recover all the damage that it has caused. He is not shocked at human failure; rather He is at home in it, drawn by it, knowing what to do about it, for He in Himself and in His blood is the answer to it all.

So it is, whenever we think of Jesus, we must think of Someone whose coming was necessitated only by the offensive business of our sin. He is firstly and lastly the answer to sin. But God, in giving Him to be the answer to our sin, has given Him to be the answer to all our other needs, both spiritual, moral, and material, for "how shall He not with Him also freely give us all things?" (Rom. 8 : 32). Jesus thus takes into Himself all the meaning of the Old Testament compound names of Jehovah, fulfilling and eclipsing them all in the final compound name He bears, JESUS, I am thy salvation.

All this implies that we must see ourselves as sinners, believers though we may be of many years standing, and that we must do so, not in a merely theoretical way, but under the searching and specific conviction of the Holy Spirit. In the pages that follow we shall come back to that again and again, for apart from seeing ourselves as sinners, we shall see no beauty in Jesus that we should desire Him (Isa. 53 : 2). He has no meaning except as the answer to sin. "To see thyself a sinner is the beginning of salvation," said St. Augustine and we may add, to continue to see ourselves as sinners is the continuance of salvation. An African, who had been convicted of sin after being a professing Christian for years, testified, "I never saw Jesus till I saw Him through my sins."

"We would see Jesus" is our theme. Seeing Him is not merely attaining an objective knowledge of Him; it is something subjective and experimental. It is seeing Him by faith to be just what I need as a sinner, a failure, a poverty-stricken

CHAPTER IV

SEEING JESUS AS THE TRUTH

WE have just seen, doubtless with gratitude, that Jesus Christ is made to us all we need. What, then, is our first and basic need? It is to know the truth—about ourselves and about God. Until we do so, we are living in a realm of illusion and we are impervious to the word of grace; it seems largely irrelevant to our case. The breaking in of the truth about ourselves and about God, and the shattering of the illusion in which we have been living, is the beginning of revival for the Christian as it is of salvation for the lost. We cannot begin to see the grace of God in the face of Jesus Christ until we have seen the truth about ourselves and given a full answer to all its challenge.

This word "truth" is an important word, especially in the writings of the Apostle John, from which much in this chapter is derived. It is one of his keywords, and in his Gospel and three Epistles it occurs no less than forty-two times. John puts truth in contrast to the lie, the devil's lie. The devil, he says, "abode not in the truth, because there is no truth in him. When he speaketh a lie, he speaketh of his own: for he is a liar, and the father of it" (John 8 : 44). This settles for us the meaning of the word, as John uses it. It is not truth in the sense of the body of Christian doctrine, but truth in the sense of honesty, reality, a revelation of things as they really are.

One of the devil's greatest weapons has always been lying propaganda. It is the way by which he conditions men to disobedience. He wove a web of lies around man in the Garden of Eden, and he has been doing so ever since. He lied to man about his perilous position as a sinner. "Ye shall not surely die" (Gen. 3 : 4), he said, "you're all right. There is nothing to worry about: you can eat of the tree with impunity." He lied also to man about God when he imputed to Him certain base motives for His prohibition with regard to the tree. "God doth know that in the day ye eat thereof . . . ye shall be as gods, knowing good and evil" (Gen. 3 : 5), he said, "He does not want you to be a god like Himself; He is keeping you down." He flattered man and maligned God. And the tragedy was that man believed the lie and acted on it, with all the tragic consequences of the Fall of man that we know.

And the devil is still weaving his web of lies about us today. He is still telling us that we are good people and devoted Christians, and that there is nothing to be concerned about in our lives. He is still telling us that God is not all that holy and uncompromising, or that God does not love us or treat us fairly. And the tragedy is that we are still believing him. The result is that we have lost sight of things as they really are, and are now living in a realm of complete illusion about ourselves.

We must not, however, blame only the devil for all this. He has a ready ally in our hearts. In the first chapter of the first Epistle of John we have the three steps in the building up of this world of illusion about ourselves. The first step is in verse 6, where we have the words, "we lie, and do not the truth". In other words, we give an impression of ourselves which is not the truth. We act a lie, even if we do not actually tell a lie. Some of us, perhaps, have been doing that for years, play-acting, wearing a mask. And little wonder, for "every one that doeth evil hateth the light, neither cometh to the light, lest his deeds should be reproved" (John 3 : 20). There is much about ourselves that we want to hide.

The next step is in verse 8, where we have the words, "We deceive ourselves, and the truth is not in us". This means that we have acted a lie for so long that we have come to believe our own lie. We begin by deceiving others, and end by deceiving ourselves. We really do believe now that we are the sort of people we have given ourselves out to be. We are quite sure that we "have never done anybody any harm" and that we are not jealous or proud as other people are, and that we are truly consecrated to the Lord. The Pharisee who thanked God that he was not as other men were, honestly thought he was telling the truth. He was, however, just as covetous, unjust, and adulterous as anybody else, but his own heart had deceived him. He was living in this same realm of illusion as we are.

The third step in the process is in verse 10, "We make Him a liar". All this leads us to the place where, when God comes to show us our sin and our real selves, we say automatically, "Not so, Lord." God, we feel, has made a mistake. He is pointing to the wrong man. Of course, we all admit theoretically we are sinners, but when God comes close, either through a message or through the faithful challenge of a friend, to show us that our hearts are "deceitful above all things, and desperately wicked" (Jer. 17 : 9) and to do so on specific points, we cannot see that it is right. However, to say that we have not sinned, when God says we have, is to make Him a liar. That is ever the end of this blindness, and while we are there God can do little further for us. We have become strangers not only to God, but also to ourselves.

It is clear, then, that our first and basic need is to be introduced to ourselves, to know the truth as God sees it.

* * * * *

It is just here that Jesus Christ is made to us what we need, for He says, "I am . . . the Truth" (John 14 : 6). In the soul's experience this is the first of His great "I am's", and our first step is to be willing to see the whole truth about ourselves and the God with whom we have to do, as it is revealed in Jesus Christ.

It is important to understand that Jesus is not saying here that He merely teaches us the truth, as if the truth were something apart from Himself; but that He Himself is the truth. Therefore, truly to see Him is to see the truth. If we are asked, Where do we see Jesus as the truth, we reply, Supremely on the Cross of Calvary. There in Him we see the whole naked truth about sin, man and the God with whom he has to do. The very scene that reveals the richest and sweetest grace of God towards man also reveals the starkest truth as to what man is. If grace flows from Calvary, so does truth, for both "grace and truth came by Jesus Christ" (John 1 : 17).

Let us try to illustrate these things at this point. It is by seeing the concern of the doctor, and the extreme measures prescribed, that the patient learns for the first time the gravity of the trouble from which he is suffering. It is by the reading of the severe sentence imposed on another man that the undiscovered law-breaker, who has been doing the same things himself but thinking lightly of them, discovers how seriously the law regards his offences. It is by seeing the suffering and sorrow undergone by a mother because of his ways that the wastrel son comes to judge the true character of those ways.

So, in like manner, Jesus says from the Cross, "See here your own condition by the shame I had to undergo for you". If the moment the Holy One took our place and bore our sins He was condemned of the Father, and left derelict in the hour of His sufferings, what must our true condition be to occasion so severe an act of judgment!

The Bible says He was made in "the likeness of sinful flesh" (Rom. 8 : 3), which means that He was there as an effigy of us. But if the moment He became that effigy, He had to cry, "My God, My God, why hast Thou forsaken Me?" (Matt. 27 : 46), what must God see us to be? It is plain that God was not forsaking the Son as the Son. He was forsaking the Son *as us*, whose likeness He was wearing. What is done to an effigy is always regarded as done to the one it represents. That derelict figure suffering under the wrath of God is ourselves, at our best as well as at our worst. There for all to see is the naked truth about the whole lot of us, Christian and non-Christian alike. If I cannot read God's estimate of man anywhere else, I can read it there. In very deed, truth, painful and humbling, has come by Jesus Christ, enough to shatter all our vain illusions about ourselves.

However, not only has the truth about ourselves come by Jesus Christ but also the truth about God and His love towards us. Left to ourselves, our guilty consciences only tell us that God is against us, that He is the God with the big stick. We see Him only as the One who sets the moral standards for us, most of them impossibly high, and therefore who cannot but censure us when we fail. There is nothing to draw us to a God like that. But the Cross of the Lord Jesus gives the lie to all this and shows us God as He really is. We see Him, not charging us with our sins, as we would have thought, but charging them to His Son for our sakes. "God was in Christ, reconciling the world unto Himself, *not imputing their trespasses unto them*" (2 Cor. 5 : 19). What we thought was the big stick was really His outstretched arm of love beckoning us back to Himself. In the face of Jesus Christ, marred for us, we see that God is not against the sinner, but for him; that He is not his enemy, but his Friend; that in Christ He has not set new and unattainable standards, but has come to offer forgiveness, peace, and new life to those who have fallen down on every standard there is. "The law was given by Moses, but grace and truth came by Jesus Christ." This is what one writer has called "the surprising generosity of the Cross". It not only surprises our guilty consciences but also melts and draws us, impelling us to return to Him in honesty and repentance, knowing that nothing but mercy is waiting for us.

*　　*　　*　　*　　*

There are no illustrations of spiritual truth like Old Testament ones; its ritual and history abound in them. Indeed, much of the ritual was instituted only to be an illustration of later New Testament truth. And we must not be thought fanciful in taking up such illustrations and using them, for the New Testament itself does so in a number of instances.

One such Old Testament illustration which the New Testament uses to show us the Lord Jesus is that contained in the Epistle to the Hebrews 13 : 11-13. "The bodies of those beasts, whose blood is brought into the sanctuary by the high priest for sin, are burned without the camp. Wherefore Jesus also, that He might sanctify the people with His own blood, suffered without the gate. Let us go forth therefore unto Him without the camp, bearing His reproach."

What would the picture of "without the camp" mean to the Hebrew Christians to whom the apostle Paul was writing? They would be taken back in imagination to the days when their nation was in the wilderness. They would visualise that great, orderly encampment, with the sacred tabernacle in the centre

of it. Around the well-defined encampment they would visualise a no man's land, known to all as "outside the camp", and
that place would be associated in their minds with certain
classes of people.

Outside the camp was where the foreigners had to live;
those who were "aliens from the commonwealth of Israel, and
strangers from the covenants of promise" (Eph. 2 : 12). Such
were not permitted normally to live within the camp.

Outside the camp, too, were the lepers. Because of the con-
tagious nature of that terrible disease, they were banished from
the camp, uncared for and excluded from all the delights open
to others.

It was also the dread place of execution for law-breakers and
criminals. According to the law of Moses, the death penalty
was to be imposed on adulterers, sabbath-breakers, idolaters
and murderers by stoning, and outside the camp was where
that took place.

In this passage, however, the apostle tells us what is perhaps
the most gruesome detail of the place. It was the place where
the bodies of those beasts whose blood had been sprinkled in
the Holy Place for sin were burnt on the refuse heap. The body
which had had symbolically placed upon it the sins of the
offerer was burnt as so much sin-cursed refuse, utterly ab-
horrent to both God and man. Day after day without the
camp the smoke was going up, and the place was pervaded by
the stench of it.

In all, that region outside the camp was not a pleasant place.
It was the place of foreigners, lepers, criminals, and sin-cursed
refuse—a place to be avoided. Yet the Scripture tells us that
it was to the spiritual counterpart of that place outside the
camp that the Lord Jesus went forth, bearing His Cross, that
He might sanctify the people with His own blood. The actual
place where He was crucified has a name as gaunt and grim
as the associations connected with outside the camp of old—
"a place of a skull" (Matt. 27 : 33). But the Gospel tells us that
the place He went to was our place, and how glibly we often
say, "He took my place!" But when we consider the place He
actually had to take for us we get a shock, for it is then we see,

as perhaps we can in no other way, what our true place is, and what our true character is before God.

First of all, then, He went for us to the place where He was a stranger, even to His Father, the place of God-forsakenness. Hanging there on the Cross, He cried, "My God, My God, why hast Thou forsaken Me?" Sin in its beginnings is the sinner forsaking God, but in its ultimate penalty it is God forsaking the sinner, and that is hell. That was the place to which Jesus went on the Cross, the place where God forsook Him. And He did so because that was our place. Ours was the curse He bore. Ours was the God-forsakenness which He endured. The logic of it all is inescapable; if the moment He took our place God forsook Him, what must our true place be before God? What truth shines from Calvary as to our dreadful condition before God!

Then, He went forth and took the place for us of a moral leper, as if He were one Himself. Indeed, that is inferred in the Scripture, "We did esteem Him stricken, smitten of God, and afflicted" (Isa. 53 : 4). Hebrew scholars suggest that the word "stricken" has the meaning of being stricken with the plague of leprosy. All through the Bible leprosy is an illustration of sin. It is a subtle disease. Beginning in a small way with only mild symptoms, it ends up as a ravaging monster, rendering the sufferer loathsome to the eye and bringing him to death. Sin, in its inception in our lives, may appear small, but in its culmination it is something utterly loathsome to both God and man, bringing the sinner to eternal separation from God. What contempt there is in the phrase "moral leper" when we refer it to another man! That was just the place the Lord Jesus was willing to take for us, that of a moral leper, loathsome to the eye of God. You ask, Why did He take so low a place? The answer is, He did so because He saw us to be just that, and He had to take that place if He was to save us. Therefore, Jesus hanging on the Cross outside the camp as a moral leper, is a declaration of my condition. If I did not know I was one in any other way I would know it by contemplating the place that Jesus had to take for me. What impurities, immoralities, and perversions stain so many lives today, yet are so carefully hidden away! But there, it is openly declared on the Cross before all men by the very place that Jesus took for us! And although we may think that these things may not have come to fruition in us as they have in others, Calvary declares that they are in us in essence and in embryo none the less.

Then, too, He went to the spiritual counterpart of that place where the criminals were stoned. "If He were not a male-factor," said the Jews to Pilate, "we would not have delivered Him up unto thee" (John 18 : 30). Jesus did not die on a bed, about which there is nothing disgraceful; He died on a Cross, and a Cross was a punishment about which there was a peculiar disgrace, for it was reserved only for criminals. Indeed, there was a criminal on either side of Him, and everybody thought that He must be one, too. They "did esteem Him stricken, smitten of God, and afflicted", because of something that He must have done, and they "hid as it were their faces from Him". And the astonishing thing is that He never disabused them. He did not say, as we would have done, "Please, oh please, do not think that I am here for anything I have done—I am here for other people's sins." Instead, He kept silent. He was willing to let them think He really was a criminal. He was willing to be "numbered with the transgressors" (Isa. 53 : 12) and to die as such, just because He saw that that was our place, and He was willing to take it for us. The Bible certainly tells us that in essence we are all criminals in God's sight. "Whosoever hateth his brother," it says, "is a murderer" (1 John 3 : 15). Anything that is not true love for my brother is hate, and hate is murder. Again we read, "Whosoever looketh on a woman to lust after her hath committed adultery with her already in his heart" (Matt. 5 : 28). God says that the lustful thought is the same in His sight as the actual deed. But even if the Bible did not say any of these things about us, we would still know they are true, and our guilt would be evident to the world, for at Calvary that fact is openly declared by Jesus dying for us.

Supremely, however, Jesus was led forth without the camp in the same way that the bodies of the sacrificial beasts were taken to be burnt, as so much sin-cursed refuse. No words can describe the moral depths which Jesus plumbed for us on the

Cross. It is not too much to say that He was dying there as so much sin-cursed refuse, and only because sin-cursed refuse is what we are seen to be in God's sight. There the smoke and stench of our sin went up from His blessed body. You and I may give one another the impression of being earnest, godly Christians, but before the Cross we have to admit that we are not that sort of person at all. At Calvary the naked truth is staring down at us all the time from the Cross, challenging us to drop the pose and own the truth.

This, then, is what Calvary shows us to be. These are not just pictures of what we were, but of what we still are, apart from Him. No matter how long we have been Christians, nor how mature we think we have become, Calvary has something fresh to show us of sin today. For sin is like an octopus. Its tentacles are everywhere. It has a thousand lives and a thousand shapes, and by perpetually changing its shape it eludes capture. If we are to see sin in all its subtle shapes and forms, and prove the power of Jesus to save us from it, we need to pray daily:

> Keep me broken, keep me watching
> At the Cross where Thou hast died.

For only there do we know our need as sinners, and therefore of Jesus.

*   *   *   *   *

What is to be our response to all this revelation of truth about ourselves and God? The sort of response that God is asking of us is very different from what one would naturally think, as will be found in John 3 : 20. The verse begins by saying, "Everyone that doeth evil hateth the light, neither cometh to the light, lest his deeds should be reproved." This means that when we have sin to hide, we shun the light, that is, everything that would expose us. Then it goes on to say, "But he that doeth truth cometh to the light, that his deeds may be made manifest, that they are wrought in God." We might have thought that if it says, "He that does evil hates the light", it would have gone on to read, "He that doeth good cometh to the light." Surely the opposite of doing evil is doing good! But that is not the contrast here. What God says is, he that doeth *truth* cometh to the light. The alternative that God presents to our doing evil is not doing good, but doing truth; that is, honesty with regard to our evil. He does not want in the first place our efforts to do good where we have done evil, to try to be kind where we have been unkind, to be friendly where we have been critical. We could do all that without any repentance for what has been there already, and without any cleansing and peace in our hearts. What God asks first of all is truth, that is, plain truthful repentance, and confession of the sin that has been committed. That will take us to the Cross of Jesus for pardon, and, where necessary, to the other whom we may have wronged, for his forgiveness, too. In that place of humble truthfulness about ourselves we shall find peace with God and man, for there we shall find Jesus afresh, and lay hold as never before on His finished work for our sin upon the Cross. Simple honesty, that is, "doing truth" about our sins, will put us right with God and man through the blood of Christ, where all the "doing good" in the world will not.

Let us welcome Jesus today as the Truth. Begin with the first thing that He is showing you. It is probably the thing that is on your mind now, even as you are reading this. The reward of your obedience to light will be more light on further sin. He does not show us ourselves all at once, for we could not bear it. But He does so progressively, as each bit of truth obeyed leads to further revelations of ourselves.

The fact that the Cross, which declares the painful truth, is also the remedy for sin, will give us a new readiness to respond to its diagnosis. If I know there is an infallible cure for a certain disease I can bear being told that I suffer from that disease. As long as I know there is a fountain for sin and uncleanness, I can face the light about myself and my sin. And the wonderful thing is that when we love the Lord Jesus as Truth we will find that He is just as precious in that relationship as in any other. It is only our dark, deceitful hearts that make us afraid of Him as Truth. He wants us to be unafraid of Him in this capacity, nay, welcoming Him. He has given us His Holy Spirit, three times called "the Spirit of Truth", to "guide us into all Truth", and we can safely put our hands in His and say, "Lord, show me all Thou dost see and all that Thou dost want me to see. I will accept it. I will not defend or argue. If Thou dost say it, then I know it is true."

CHAPTER V

SEEING JESUS AS THE DOOR

WHAT we have seen of the Lord Jesus as the awesome truth about ourselves and our sins prepares us for the next sight of Him, the sight which the Holy Spirit longs to give to the convicted heart—that of the Lord Jesus as the Door. Such a sight of ourselves as we have had must give the convicted heart a sense of utter exclusion from a Holy God. If that is what we have been like all the time, and if those are the sins to which we have been blind for so long, little wonder, then, that God has seemed so far from us, that our hearts have been cold and that our Christian service has seemed hard and barren. We need look no farther for the cause of the deadness that reigns in our fellowship and our churches. Not only does the soul see itself rightfully excluded because of its sin but, knowing its weakness, it wonders if there can be a way to God that a person with a heart like his can tread.

Here the Lord Jesus presents Himself to us as just what we need, and confronts us with another great "I am". Says He, "I am the Door: by Me if any man enter in, he shall be saved" (John 10 : 9). If the deceived need to see the truth, the excluded need to find a door, and Jesus is both—Truth to the deceived and Door to the excluded. He is the Door to revival and every other blessing for the Christian as He is the Door to salvation for the lost—and a Door, moreover, as easily accessible to the weakest and most failing as to the most saintly.

The very fact that the Lord Jesus said He was the Door presupposes that there is a wall, a barrier, which excludes us from God. There is indeed. Who of us has not found it so? It has withstood our most earnest moral endeavours and thwarted our every resolution. We go to pray, but it is there. We seek His help, but it is still there. Our very worship of Him is ever from a distance. Only those who have never seriously set themselves to seek God can imagine there is no such barrier. The Bible tells us the nature of this barrier. It tells us it is sin, and only sin, that separates man and God (Isa. 59 : 2) By sin, it means the attitude of self-centredness, and independence of God which is common to us all, and the many acts of transgression which have issued from it. It is because "we have followed too much the devices and desires of our own hearts" that "we have offended against His holy laws". And sin always builds a wall between us and God.

This wall has not always been there. It was erected only with the first act of transgression. Only then did man want to hide from God. Only then did God in justice have to set the Cherubim and the flaming sword to bar the way back to the Tree of Life (Gen. 3 : 24). Since then, all Adam's descendants have been born on the other side of that flaming sword, in the "far country" of separation from God into which the first prodigal, father of them all, went. And there men remain until their eyes are opened to see the one Door back which God has provided for them.

I found myself speaking one day to a woman in a counselling room after one of the great Crusade meetings which have been held in Britain in recent years. She told me that she had come forward because her son of sixteen had done so. I said, "But what about you?" She replied, "Oh, I've always been a Christian." The moment she said that, I knew she had never been a Christian at all. No one has "always been a Christian", but rather always a sinner, always separated from God by sin until saved by Divine grace. Mere human religiousness does nothing to restore us.

Let us not think that this separating power of sin applies only to those who have never known Christ personally. Those of us who have passed initially through the Door back to God know all too often the wall that sin can still erect between the soul and God. Though we have been restored from the "far country " of original sin, sin may yet come in, perhaps in more subtle forms, and we find ourselves as a result in other "far countries", smaller but none the less real—the "far country" of jealousy, or of resentment, or of self-pity, or of compromise with the world. And there always arises "a mighty famine in that land" (Luke 15 : 14), as it did for the Prodigal Son, and we begin to be in want. It is "not a famine of bread, nor a thirst for water, but of hearing the words of the Lord" (Amos 8 : 11). Who of us does not know the coldness of heart towards the Lord, the apparent deadness of the Sacred Page and the accumulating defeats in other areas of life because of the barrier that sin in one particular area has brought between us and God? We are not suggesting that the new-born child of God loses his place in the family of God because of sin that has come in, but he does lose his fellowship with his heavenly Father, and then famine conditions invariably obtain in his heart until he repents.

In those famine conditions, however, the Christian is all too often blind to the real sin or sins that have separated him from God, and therefore he attempts to deal only with the famine itself rather than with its causes. He may resolve to pray more or to serve God more faithfully. Or he may "join himself to a citizen of that country" (Luke 15 : 15), as the prodigal did, and make worldly alliances in the hope of bringing back a little pleasure to his now joyless heart. All such efforts will always prove futile, and God uses that experience ultimately to show him that it is with sin that he must deal, and what that sin is.

However, even when a man knows the sins that have separated him from God, he occupies himself so often with the problem of how not to sin again rather than with getting back to God and to peace. It is frankly too late for such considerations. Sin has come in and done its damage. Even if we "get the victory" and never do that thing again, that fact would never bring us back to rest and joy. The simple truth is that words such as "Jesus satisfies" and "He gives the victory" just do not apply when we are in the far country. All that, and much more, awaits us only upon our return to the Father's house.

It is just here that we flounder for lack of knowing how to get back; how to get through the many barriers that sin has brought. If we knew this, we would be radiantly happy souls indeed. Sin, though it might come, would not defeat us with despair and deadness of spirit, for we would know a sure way into freedom and joy again, and we could avail ourselves of it just as often as we needed to. Truly our need, then, is to see a door.

This is the point at which the Lord Jesus meets us again. To the enquiring heart who would ask Him to show him the Door, He says in effect, "If ye had known Me, ye should have known the Door also. He that hath seen Me, hath seen the Door. I am the Door, by Me if any man enter he shall be saved." Jesus does not merely show us the Door; He Himself is the Door. This is God's great gift of love to a prodigal world that still has its back to Him—a never-failing Door back to peace and satisfaction, if we will but turn and see Him standing so near and accessible to us. And such a Door is He, that neither preparatory steps nor subsequent steps are necessary to enter into what we need. In simply coming to Him we *have* passed from one spiritual condition to another, for He is Himself both the blessing needed and the Door to it. It is just such a picture of Him as the door that we have in the well-known hymn which begins,

> Out of my bondage, sorrow and night,
> Jesus, I come! Jesus, I come!
> Into Thy freedom, gladness and light,
> Jesus, I come to Thee!

This picture gives us the basic word of the Gospel of Christ. The Gospel does not call us to try to be *like* Christ, but rather to come *through* Christ. We are presented with a door rather than an example. Again and again we find Paul's Epistles punctuated with the phrase, "through Jesus Christ our Lord" (Rom. 6 : 23 and similar verses) or its equivalent. He never mentions a blessing or an experience of good that God has for us, but that he hastens to add "through Jesus Christ our Lord". And rightly so, for what use is a delectable garden or a handsome house if there is no open gate or door by which to get there? This is what disappointed Christians are asking for all the time. "It is all right to talk about this wonderful life of fellowship with God," they say, "but how does a man like me get there? I have tried so often." Jesus delights to tell us, "I am how you get there! I am the Door." There is no blessing that God has for us, be it salvation, victory, peace of heart, or revival, but that God has provided an easily accessible Door to it in His Son.

*   *   *   *   *

If we are truly to see the Lord Jesus as our Door and to experience the blessedness of it, there are four essential things which we must understand about Him in that capacity.

First, we must see Him as the *open* Door, wide open! How easy it is to see Him as something other than that! There are times when some of us seem to see Him as little more than the One who sets the standard, who delineates the path of duty and who only censures us when we do not attain it. That is to make Him but another Moses, who only causes us to despair, and if we see Him as a Door at all, it is only as a shut Door. But that is not the Jesus from heaven. "The law was given by Moses" and condemned the whole lot of us, "but grace and truth came by Jesus Christ" (John 1 : 17). If grace is God's goodness to those who do not deserve it, that means He is an open Door through which sinners may come. The hour of its opening was that hour when, hanging upon the Cross, He cried in triumph, " 'It is finished': and He bowed His head and gave up the ghost" (John 19 : 30). As if to make quite clear what was being accomplished out there on Calvary, the veil of the temple, which for centuries had hung as an excluding barrier between the Holy of Holies and the rest of the temple, was rent at that very moment from top to bottom. In that way the separating barrier of sin between man and God was declared breached, and the Door for sinful man declared open. We are now urged to have "boldness to enter the Holiest by the blood of Jesus, by a new and living Way", for the blood of Jesus Christ tells us that all the judgment due to our sin was exhausted on the Cross. When we truly see that, even the most self-condemned have boldness to come.

This means that there is now no barrier or obstacle between man and God. What appear to be the obstacles—man's coldness, unbelief, and such sins—are the very things that qualify him for this Door, provided he will acknowledge them, for it is a Door for people who are characterised by just such sins. We cannot suppress or conquer these things, but we can judge them as sin and bring them to Jesus. And as we do so, what appeared to be an all-excluding wall is found to be in Him an open door, and we have passed into peace and fellowship with God.

Second, we need to see this Door as open *on street level*, that is, open for the failure *as a failure*, and not merely for us when we have become a little more successful. The Jews in the New Testament could easily believe that there was salvation for the Gentile, if he was circumcised and became a Jew. What they could not and would not believe was that there was salvation for the Gentile *as a Gentile*, without becoming a Jew at all. This was the controversy that dogged Paul's steps all his years. He insisted all the way through that the Gentile could be saved as a Gentile, and the sinner as a sinner, without anything to commend him to God but the blood of Jesus Christ (Gal. 2 : 14–16, etc.). In other words, he insisted on seeing Christ as the Door open on street level.

We Christians would not think of going back on the Gospel committed to Paul as concerns "them that are without", at least, not in theory. But when we think of our own deep needs and failures, and when we pray about being used of God and when we ask God for revival, we put the door for ourselves somewhere higher than on street level. Here we instinctively feel that the failure cannot be blessed as a failure, but only as a better Christian, and so we try to make ourselves such. We succeed only in putting the door just beyond our reach, for it is the becoming that little bit better that defies us. And all the time the Door is open on street level, the level of our shame and failure, and all that is needed is the willingness to acknowledge that such is our true condition, and to come in faith to Jesus.

We sometimes talk about the price of revival, and we need to be very careful as to what we mean when we speak like this. We may place that price so high that we put revival right beyond the reach of the ordinary run of mortals. Maybe that is our way of attempting to justify God, that He has not yet, apparently, given the revival His people need. But that is a wrong done to God and a cruelty done to His Church. There is without doubt a price to be paid for revival, but it is not of necessity the price of long nights of prayer or excruciating sacrifices, but of simply humbling pride to repent of sin. The Door is open on street level to revival as it is to salvation and every other blessing. In coming to Him in repentance we come into Revival, for He is Himself Revival and the simple Door to it. If it is contended that this is not the widespread, spectacular revival which is written about and which is needed today, we can only say that such a movement has always begun this way—with God being allowed to deal with one person, and with that person giving his testimony. May it not be that the reason why God has not blessed us with revival as we have wanted it, is that we have sought it, not by faith, but by the works of the law (Rom. 9 : 32)—we have missed the door on street level? And may it not be that we have been expecting to "see revival" in others, rather than being willing to be personally revived ourselves and be the first to admit our need of this? Is it not significant that when there is patently an experience of revival in lives, those revived do not talk about revival but rather about Jesus?

The glorious truth is that Christ is immediately available to us, as we are, and where we are. God has made Him as accessible to us sinners as He possibly can. Listen to the apostle Paul on this point. "The righteousness which is of faith speaketh on this wise, 'Say not in thine heart, Who shall ascend into heaven? (that is, to bring Christ down from above:) or, Who shall descend into the deep? (that is, to bring up Christ again from the dead.)' But what saith it? 'The word is nigh thee, even in thy mouth, and in thy heart:' that is, the word of faith, which we preach" (Rom. 10 : 6-8). It is not a matter of straining to attain the heights, nor artificially trying to abase ourselves to the depths. His blood has made Him available to the sinner *as a sinner*, and to the failing saint *as a failing saint*, if he will only admit that that is what he is. The word which we need, therefore, to contact Him is right in our mouth and in our heart, the simple word of confession and faith.

This leads to the next sight that we must have of this

wonderful Door opened at the Cross. It is *a low Door*, that is, we have to bow our heads low in repentance if we are to enter by it. Scripture mentions again and again the disease (if we may call it that) of the "stiff neck". It is a figurative way of speaking of man's self-will and stubbornness, shown especially in his unwillingness to admit himself wrong. Sometimes you can feel your neck going almost literally stiff when someone accuses you and you resent it! When our necks are like that, and our wills unbroken to acknowledge our sin, we can never enter by that Door. We just hit our heads against the lintel! He bowed His head on the Cross for us (John 19 : 30), and we shall have to bow our heads low in self-judgment and repentance of sin if we are to know the power of His blood to cleanse and bring us into rest.

So often the way in which we repent to God and sometimes apologise to another for a wrong shows that we have not truly judged ourselves. We betray the fact that we feel it is only an unfortunate slip, and that we have on this occasion acted out of character with our true selves. What deception! The truth is we have not acted out of character at all, but in accordance with our true form, as declared to us by that Figure hanging on the Cross for us! Sometimes we should do well to add, when we are putting something right with another, "So you see what I really am." The head must be bowed low to the dust to admit that we are no better than what Jesus had to become for us. Then we find Him a Door indeed.

Then we must understand that this Door is *a narrow Door*. "Narrow is the gate, and straitened the way, that leadeth unto life" (Matthew 7 : 14 R.V.). At first the road to the Cross seems broad, and we can all go together. But as we get nearer to that place of repentance the path gets narrower. There is not room for us all abreast. We can no longer be lost in the crowd. Others fall behind. At last when we come to the One who is the Door Himself, there is not room even for two, you and that other one. If you are going to enter, you will have to stand there utterly alone. It must be you alone who repents, without waiting for any other. But we do not want to be the one to repent. The devil tells us that the other by our side is so very wrong, and he makes us unwilling to repent unless they repent first. But men never get through the Door that way! You must be the one to repent and to do so first, as if you were the only sinner in the world. The other may be wrong, but your reactions to their wrong (reactions of, perhaps, resentment, criticism, or unforgiveness) are wrong too, and in God's sight more culpably so. For "Thou shalt love thy neighbour as thyself" is second only to "Thou shalt love the Lord thy God with all thy heart" (Matt. 22 : 37), and those reactions in your heart are not love.

Jesus never fails as a Saviour when we come to Him as sinners. But if in any degree we are not finding Him a real Saviour who brings us fully out of darkness and defeat into light and liberty, it is because on one point or another we are not willing to be broken and see ourselves as sinners.

*   *   *   *   *

We are now in a position to look at a final picture the Lord gives us in John 10—this time not so much of the Door but of the way in which we so often miss it. Said He, "He that entereth not by the door, but climbeth up some other way, the same is a thief and a robber" (John 10 : 1). The first interpretation of this word concerns the false teacher who seeks entrance to the sheepfold as a shepherd, but only to the enrichment of himself and the destruction of the sheep. However, as we look at this man trying to get into the sheepfold by painfully and slowly climbing up the wall, we may see that from another point of view this is an illustration of what we so often do. He has his fingers and toes in the crevices as he tensely struggles up. Every now and then he falls to the bottom and has to start climbing again. After repeated failures he is in despair that he will ever reach the top and thus get into the sheepfold. But all the time, there is the door open for him at street level. Either he has not seen it or he is unwilling to make use of it. Perhaps it is the latter, for he could not enter by that door as a self-styled shepherd, but only as a repentant sheep.

What a picture this is of the grievous mistake we so often make in our anxiety to get into an experience of salvation or sanctification or revival or some other blessing of which we stand in need! We are not entering by the Door, but are striving to climb up some other way—by the way of self-improvement, turning over a new leaf, determining to have longer devotions, trying to witness more, and so on. We see the standard of the victorious life above us, and we are quite sure that if we can attain to it in this or that particular we shall be in fellowship with God and filled with His Spirit. But it is the attaining to it which all the time defeats us. And all the time we are climbing so hard the Lord Jesus stands immediately available to us as our Door, open on street level, and we could so quickly enter in if we were willing to bow our heads at His Cross. All the different and subtle ways by which we try to climb up some other way are but variants of the way of works which God has declared can never bring us into rest (Eph. 2 : 8, 9).

It may be asked, Is it wrong to do such things as have been mentioned? Of course not; they are to have an essential part in every Christian life. But they are valueless if what God is asking us at the moment is to repent about something. Unconfessed sin vitiates all our religious exercises; even as it is written, "To what purpose is the multitude of your sacrifices unto Me? . . . Your hands are full of blood" (Isa. 1 : 11, 15). But the human heart would much rather offer to God its works, no matter how costly, than humble itself to confess sin. That is the reason why man is always predisposed to go the way of works; he does not want to bow his head to go through the Door. That is the reason, also, why God has rejected the way of salvation by works or sanctification by works; the way of works is so often but a substitute for repentance. "Thou desirest not sacrifice; else would I give it. The sacrifices of God are a broken spirit" (Psa. 51 : 16, 17), and that spirit always finds its way through the Door.

Yet another reason why God rejects the way of works as a means to enter into blessing is that it makes Christ of none effect to us (Gal. 5 : 4). Said Paul, "If righteousness (or any other blessing) come by the law, then Christ is dead in vain" (Gal. 2 : 21). The more tense and striving I become in my

CHAPTER VI

SINAI OR CALVARY?

IT would seem from what we have read in the foregoing chapter that it is simplicity itself for us to enter by the Door which is the Lord Jesus. However, Satan knows how to beset us round with subtle difficulties when, under conviction of sin and out of touch with God, we would long to find peace and freedom. Therefore, before going on to consider that into which the Door leads us, we must pause in this chapter to try to help the convicted soul in some of the battles that go on in his heart just outside the Door.

Whenever a sense of sin lies upon our conscience, two Persons, it seems, fight to get hold of that conviction—the devil and the Holy Spirit. The devil wants to get hold of it in order to take it and us to Sinai, and there condemn us and bring us into bondage. The Holy Spirit, however, wants to take us and our sin to Calvary, there to bring us through the Door into peace and freedom. These two places represent for us the two covenants; the one from "Mount Sinai, which gendereth to bondage" (Gal. 4 : 24)—the covenant of law; and the other—the covenant of grace, wrought out and sealed for us by the death of the Lord Jesus on Calvary. The devil seeks to take us to the one, and the Holy Spirit to the other. Put like that, the issues seem simple, but in practice the mischievous thing is that the devil often simulates the voice of the Holy Spirit in order that the uninstructed Christian will think it is God who is taking him to the place of condemnation and bondage, and that therefore he must follow.

Mount Sinai was, of course, the historical place where God gave the Ten Commandments (Exod. 20). Ten times God spake out of the cloud and fire, and each time it was to announce a great moral commandment binding upon man— "Thou shalt" and "Thou shalt not". There the basic covenant of law was given by which man's relationship with God was to be governed. Put quite simply, it was, "This do and thou shalt live", and "This fail to do, and thou shalt die". That is still the covenant that the heart of man finds it easiest to understand, and to which his conscience most readily responds. In ordinary life today it represents for us the whole system of moral and religious standards that each man has worked out for himself as a result of the moral light which has played upon his life from various sources.

Now, when a sense of failure of some sort lies upon the conscience, the devil immediately endeavours to take us to the law, that which we have called Sinai, in order to accuse us with regard to the standards we have adopted there, but which we have failed to keep. The higher our moral and spiritual standards, the more there is for the devil to accuse us. He is rightly called "the accuser of our brethren" (Rev. 12 : 10). He not only accuses us to God, but he accuses the Christian to himself, and he does so by pointing to all the matters, real or imaginary, in which the Christian is failing to keep the law which he has espoused, and he thus produces in him a sense of condemnation. This is what the psychiatrist diagnoses in his neurotic patient as a "guilt complex", but it is also something that many a healthy-minded Christian carries around with him all too often. The source of it all is the devil, and that which gives strength to his accusations is clearly the law. This sheds light on Paul's words, "The strength of sin is the law" (1 Cor. 15 : 56).

These accusations have usually two effects upon the Christian, and they are precisely the effects which the devil designs to produce. First, they cause in him the reaction of self-excuse. In the Epistle to the Romans there is the statement, "Their thoughts the mean while accusing or else excusing one another" (Rom. 2 : 15). To excuse ourselves and to assert our innocence is ever the natural reaction to accusation; and this is exactly what the devil wants us to do. By his accusations he has provoked us to try to stand before God on the ground of our own righteousness and innocence; and he knows, and we ought to know too, that there is nothing for us on that ground. All that God has for sinners, He has for them on the condition that they will acknowledge that that is what they really are. And so our thoughts go round and round, one half of us accusing ourselves, and the other half excusing ourselves, and all the time that we are thus excusing ourselves, we are getting farther and farther from the grace of God and from peace. This was precisely the effect that the accusations of his friends had on Job. In suggesting that his trials came as a result of some wrong in him, they provoked him to assert vigorously his innocence, and on that ground he found that God fought against him. Upright man that he really was, he had none the less to be broken to accept the sinner's place before he could be at peace with God again.

The second effect of the devil's accusations is to cause us to get on to the ground of self-effort and "striving". He tells us what we are not, in order to get us to struggle in our own strength to make up for it. He accuses us that we are not praying enough, or not speaking enough to others of their need of Christ, or not giving enough to God, or that we are not humble enough, and so on, simply in order to get us to attempt to do all those things in the energy of self. The whole purpose of the devil in these accusations is to get us into striving and self-effort, and thus into real bondage. In that condition he has got us trying to "climb up some other way" into blessing (and a hard, painful business it is, for the wall is high!) instead of entering in by the Door, open on street level. And he can do all this under the guise of being the voice of God to us. But he is "a liar, and the father of it" (John 8 : 44). His accusations, though they have the appearance of truth and of being based on the law of God, are but half-truths, and all the more dangerous for that reason.

How we need to discern the voice of the devil, and to know in experience God's answer to the thunderings of Mount Sinai against us! It is to reveal just that to us, that the Holy Spirit has come.

*   *   *   *   *

If the devil wants to reach that sense of sin that lies upon our conscience, so does the Holy Spirit. But how differently

He works! He takes that sin, and us with it, to Calvary, to Jesus our Door. There He shows us that that sin, and much else, was anticipated and settled by the Lord Jesus in His death upon the Cross. Whether what the devil says to us is true or false is all settled by the Lord Jesus for us. The worst that the devil can say about us is not to be compared to the dark depths of sin that swept over Him there. At the Cross the most self-condemned finds nothing but forgiveness, cleansing, and comfort. The fact, then, that we are the sinners we are, of which the devil loves to accuse us, is only a half-truth. The other half of the truth is that Jesus died for us and did a complete work for us. That is something the devil never tells us. Only the gentle Holy Spirit tells us that. Indeed, it is His great delight to "comfort all that mourn" (Isa. 61 : 2) and to do so by giving us a fresh sight of Jesus and His blood, and of His appearing even now in the presence of God for us.

This revelation has two effects on the believer when he truly sees it—the exact opposite of the two effects of the accusations of Satan, which have already been mentioned. First, he freely acknowledges his sin, and judges himself. If the accusations of Satan had the effect of causing him to excuse himself, and protest his innocence, the grace of God revealed at Calvary has the effect of causing him to admit his sin. He is not even at too great pains to sort out what may be a true accusation and what may be false; the answer in the blood of Christ is the same in either case. Furthermore, if he could regard himself innocent on one score, there are many others on which he is hopelessly guilty. In any case, it ill befits him to be attempting to prove his innocence on even one point before the Cross, where the Wholly Just died as the Wholly Unjust for him. Thus there is produced in him that attitude of heart which in the sight of God is of great price, the attitude of the broken and contrite heart. The moment he adopts this attitude he is brought right on to redemption ground, where nothing but grace is lavished upon him by God.

Second, the sight of Calvary and its meaning for him provokes him not only freely to admit his sin, but also to rest from self-initiated activity to get himself right. Perhaps no verse expresses more clearly this effect of our coming to the Cross than one in Isaiah where it says, "In returning and rest shall ye be saved" (Isa. 30 : 15). The situation in this thirtieth chapter of Isaiah was that Israel was in a serious plight, with her enemies descending on her from the north. In this plight she resorted to alliances with other nations, in particular with Egypt, to whom she sent her ambassadors for help. Into this scene Isaiah steps with the word, "Woe to the rebellious children, saith the Lord, that take counsel, but not of Me". He declares that "the Egyptians shall help in vain, and to no purpose", for the root cause of their predicament is their departure from the Lord; it is for this cause that God has brought upon them the armies of Babylon, that He might humble and chasten them. He therefore calls upon them to return to the Lord in repentance. To this the people might well have replied, "To return to the Lord is all very well, but what relevance has it to a situation like ours in which we are besieged by our foes?" And Isaiah would doubtless have said, "It has every relevance, for in dealing with your wrong relationship with God you are dealing with the root cause of all your present troubles." "But," they might have replied, "what are we to do about the armies of Babylon?" "If you return to the Lord," he would have answered, *"you can rest about that,* for God will never fail to work for those who, having repented, rest in quiet confidence in His overruling and restoring grace." This, then, is something of the background and meaning of this great word to them, "In returning and rest shall ye be saved".

The same word is for us, too. Having returned, that is, having repented, we can rest, and we can do so because we see that Jesus has done a finished work for us on the Cross. We can rest, first, about our righteousness, which has received such a damaging blow both in our eyes and in the eyes of others by the sin that we are having to repent of. We see that the precious blood of Jesus has anticipated and settled the very sin we are confessing, and has provided a perfect righteousness for us before God, and we can rest content to have none other before men. Indeed, it is not until we are content to have no other righteousness before both God and men that we find peace. But then, when we do, what rest is ours from futile efforts to justify ourselves! We can say, "If others think me a failure, they think the truth—but a failure who has found peace through the blood of His Cross", and we are prepared to give them just that testimony. We have learnt at last to overcome Satan by the blood of the Lamb, and by the word of our testimony (Rev. 12 : 11), and our hearts are free. We stand before God and move amongst men with the witness:

> This is all my righteousness,
> Nothing but the blood of Jesus.

More than that, having returned, we can rest about the consequences of our sin, and about the situation in which it may have involved us. Up to the moment of our repentance the situation in which we have involved ourselves is our responsibility. We have made our bed and we must lie in it, or, more likely, do our frenzied best to get ourselves out of it. But the moment we repent and put the blame where it belongs, on ourselves, the all-availing blood of Jesus comes into view on our behalf before God, and He then is pleased for Christ's sake to make the tangled situation His own responsibility, and we can rest about it. He first gives the repentant one peace through the blood, and then deals with his situation. As someone has said, "God forgives the messer, and unmesses the mess", or rather, He makes the mess the raw material for a fresh purpose of love.

This is the vision of grace which was given Jeremiah as he watched the potter at work (Jer. 18 : 1-6). When the potter saw the vessel marred in his hand he might well have discarded it. Instead, "he made it again another vessel, as seemed good to the potter to make it". So does God delight to do with all our marred vessels when we truly humble ourselves, be the marred vessel our whole life or just a day in that life, be it a complex set of circumstances or just a relationship with one other person which we have spoiled. And as we rest as repentant ones at the Cross and take whatever steps He may show us to be necessary, we watch Him bringing a new purpose

to birth, His order comes out of our chaos, and we are left with
nothing but adoring praise to Him. The new purpose He works
may not be unmixed with discipline, but grace assures us it is
going to be one of infinite good, and so we rest.

So it is that the value of the blood of Christ extends not only
to our sin but also to the circumstances connected with our sin.
This is a sight of the power of the blood of Christ which brings
infinite relief and peace to the tortured, remorseful soul and
which causes him to rest indeed from his anxieties to prove the
grace of His wonderful God.

*   *   *   *   *

The same word of rest applies to our dealing with the
qualities we know we lack in our lives. We are convicted that
we lack love for somebody, or that we lack faith in a certain
matter, or that we have been prayerless. As we have seen, the
devil wants to accuse us of these things in order to provoke us
to strive to make up for them in our own strength. But the
Holy Spirit takes us with our conviction to Calvary to provoke us to repent about them and then—rest about them.

So often, however, it would seem that we are reading this
verse as it were "in returning and resolving ye shall be saved".
Knowing that we are not loving towards somebody, we try
to be more loving. Aware that we lack faith in a matter, we
struggle to trust more. Convicted that we have not been praying as we should, we make resolutions as to how long we shall
spend on our devotions each day in the future. The trouble
with all this is that it is we who are doing it all, and it is not the
work of Christ. As we know, or ought to know, "that in me
(that is, in my flesh) dwelleth no good thing", we can be almost
certain that very little will come of it.

The Holy Spirit, however, is not concerned primarily to get
us to try to be better, but to repent deeply of the sin there is;
not to try to be more loving to that person, but to repent of
having been jealous and critical towards him and so on. Then,
having repented, the Holy Spirit would bid us rest as sinners
at the Cross, where sin is cleansed away, and so be at peace.
As we rest as sinners in that low place, Jesus pours into our

hearts His own love for that other person, a love that will sometimes send us to that person to put things right with them, and He gives us a forbearance towards them that was never there before. In that low place where we confess our worry, He gives us His own faith, "the faith of the Son of God" (Gal. 2 : 20). There, too, He will lead us to those devotions which He wants on each occasion. So it is, instead of trying to "climb up some other way" into victory, we enter into it by the Door, as we bow in repentance at His Cross. In this way we find the reality of "Not I, but Christ liveth in me", for it is into His love, patience, and victory that we enter, not ours. And so it is that we learn by experience, "In returning and rest shall ye be saved".

An illustration will help at this point to make clear the application of the principles involved in the words, "In returning and rest shall ye be saved". At a certain place in East Africa, which had been a very real centre of revival, a time of spiritual coldness had come, and the one-time joyous testimony seemed to have died from among the fellowship of those who met there. This was known and acknowledged by the Christians, but the spiritual famine seemed to continue. Then there came among them an African Christian from another part, a man full of zeal and one who thought he "knew all the answers". He charged them with their coldness and said, "Little wonder, when the township next to you is completely pagan and you are doing nothing to preach the Gospel there." He urged them to get busy and conduct open-air meetings there. A godly leader in the local group answered him with great wisdom along these lines. "You are quite right—we are cold. We have acknowledged that to God and have been repenting. But we are not going to start striving to do this or that to bring the blessing back, not even street preaching. Having repented, we are going to rest as sinners under the blood of Jesus until God is pleased to meet us again." Sure enough, God soon met them, and the Holy Spirit began to work again in their midst, and each was able to praise again for fresh sights of Jesus. Their cups were so full that when they went to that pagan township to make their purchases they could not but witness of Jesus to those they met in the shops and elsewhere. And ere long, a man was saved, and then another, and then another, and a work of grace began in that place. Thus they discovered the efficacy of the way of repentance and rest, for it brought Jesus Himself into their situation; and they were enabled to take that way only because they saw the efficacy of His finished work on the Cross for them.

* * * * *

How differently, then, does the Holy Spirit work from the devil. While Satan accuses only to bring despair, bondage, and striving, the Holy Spirit convicts only to bring comfort, freedom, and rest. Indeed, it is by discerning this fact that we can learn to distinguish between the accusing of Satan and the conviction of the Holy Spirit. If the reproof is of a nagging nature, that is, blaming, without any end to it, and if it is a vague and general reproof, rather than clearly specific, then we may know it to be, as a rule, the accusation of Satan. If the reproof is clear and specific, and if we instinctively know that we have only to be willing to say, "Yes", and repent, to have peace and comfort, then we may be assured that it is the voice of the gracious Holy Spirit, and we may safely obey His convictions, and turn to Calvary.

> Under the law with its ten-fold lash,
> Learning, alas, how true,
> That the more I tried the sooner I died,
> While the law cried, You! You!! You!!!
>
> Hopelessly still did the battle rage,
> "O wretched man" my cry,
> And deliverance I sought by some penance bought,
> While my soul cried, I! I!! I!!!
>
> Then came a day when my struggling ceased,
> And trembling in every limb,
> At the foot of the Tree where One died for me,
> I sobbed out, HIM! HIM!! HIM!!!

CHAPTER VII

SEEING JESUS AS THE WAY

THE picture of the Lord Jesus as the Door properly belongs to the beginning of the Christian life. It is pre-eminently the message which the unregenerate man needs to hear when, under conviction of sin, he desires to return to God and find salvation. We have, however, applied this picture of the Door in a previous chapter to the needs of the believer, because he is sometimes so cold and defeated, and has been so for so long, that when ultimately he gets right with the Lord the entrance into more abundant life is an important crisis for him. In any case, the principles of grace revealed by the Door are for him ever afterwards. The entrance for him into every further blessing is "through Jesus Christ our Lord" and must be entered by repentance and faith. It will, however, save the reader from confusing the imagery if, as he reads the present chapter, he regards the picture of the Door as applying either to the beginning of the Christian life or to some further crisis experience. What follows now applies to the Christian life itself after entrance by the Door, and is concerned with how to continue in the experience of grace into which we have entered.

Now, what lies beyond the Door? Scripture could have pictured the Door leading us into a house or a garden. If it had done so, we would have gathered that the Lord Jesus brings us into a static experience of salvation, peace, and holiness, and that once having entered in, we would more or less stay there, enjoying it all without continuous co-operation on our part.

Scripture, however, gives us the picture of the Door leading us, not into a house, but on to a *Way*. Said the Lord Jesus, "Narrow is the Gate, and straitened the Way that leadeth unto life" (Matt. 7 : 14 R.V.). The Gate opens on to a Way that stretches right ahead. And the Lord Jesus who had said, "I am the Door", now says, "I am the Way" (John 14 : 6) that lies beyond the Door. Both Door and Way are the same blessed Person.

Now a Way speaks not of a final, settled blessing but rather of a walk, of an experience which is continuous. A walk is simply a reiterated step, where something is happening each moment in the present; after one step, the next step; after the one "now", the next "now". This illustrates the fact that our experience of Christ is to be a continuous present tense, a glorious "now". This moment we are to be at peace with God through Him; and after this moment, the next moment in living fellowship with Him, and thus the next moment and so on. Here, past crises do not help us. The Door experience was essential, but is now past. We may be able to testify that we were saved or sanctified on such a date, but God does not want us to be continually harking back to that in our mind, but to be living with Him each moment in the present, where He will be to us all we need.

Now a walk like that requires that there should be a way on which to walk. As we drive easily along our modern paved highways we can hardly imagine the almost impassable terrain that confronted our fathers when they sought to make their way through a country where there were no roads. Whenever an undeveloped country is being opened up, the first thing to be done is always to build highways. The best automobiles in the world are valueless without such roads. And we have only to contemplate for a moment the fact that we are called to walk in continuous, present-tense fellowship with God to find ourselves asking, How? How can people like ourselves, in circumstances like those in which we are, enjoy a continuous walk like that? With evil propensities within us, and sin around us, we are faced with what looks like an impassable swamp. We need a Way, and a Way of such an order that foolish way-faring men like ourselves may walk thereon in peace and safety.

God has provided for us such a Way. He who provided for

us the Door has not failed to provide the Way we so much need after we have entered by the Door. It was foretold long before, and prophets like Isaiah eagerly looked forward to it. Said he, "And an Highway shall be there, and a Way, and it shall be called the Way of Holiness: the unclean shall not pass over it . . . but the redeemed shall walk there" (Isa. 35 : 8). That Way consecrated for people like ourselves is the Lord Jesus Himself, for He said, "I am the Way." On either side are the swamps of sin, but stretching through them and above them is our Highway, exactly suited to our faltering feet, the Lord Jesus Himself.

This was the conception that the early Christians had of the Christian life. In the Acts of the Apostles they always referred to what they had found in the Lord Jesus as a Way. On no less than six occasions Christianity is referred to there as "this Way" (Acts 9 : 2; 19 : 9, 23; 22 : 4; 24 : 14, 22).* Indeed, in that book it bears no other name. To them Jesus was not only their Door, but their Way, on whom and with whom they were continuously and delightedly walking.

The Door, then, speaks of the beginning or the crisis, while the Way speaks of the going on. Both are fully provided for in the Lord Jesus.

Now if there is one thing more important than entering by the Door, it is going on in the Way. Having entered by the Door, the walk is going to occupy us right to the end of our days. But it is just this which is our greatest difficulty. Compared with the ease with which we entered by the Door, the walk seems hard indeed. It seems difficult to maintain that fresh fellowship with God which was so vivid when we began. It is hard to maintain His peace in our hearts. It seems difficult to make the means of grace work; and prayer, the Bible, and worship become unreal to us. We find it difficult to be effective witnesses for Christ, and to manifest the sweetness and holiness we should. The truth is that many of us who have entered by the Door are not really walking the Way at all, though we still have our faces Zionwards. We have slipped off the Highway

* The R.V. brings out "this Way" even more clearly in these verses than the Authorised Version.

that has been divinely cast up, and are painfully dragging our steps through the swamp that abounds on either side. Sometimes I have heard a Christian apply to himself the expressive word "stuck" when he is in that condition.

Basically this difficulty is due to the fact that we are not seeing Jesus as the Way, but are trying to make other things the way, and they just do not work. Some feel that prayer is the most important thing in the Christian life, and it becomes the way for them. Others would put Bible study in that place, others fellowship, others personal witnessing, yet others the Church and the Sacraments, and yet others Christian neighbourliness. It is felt that if we do these things, then we shall be really living the full Christian life, and we thus make them the Way.

None of these things, however, is the Way, and they only make the Christian life hard and barren when we try to make them such, even in a small degree. First, they have no answer to sin, and sin is the Christian's problem all the time. Satan knows how to provoke our hearts to wrong reactions. Prayer, witnessing, fellowship, church going, and so on do not cleanse sin nor give the guilty conscience peace. That which does not anticipate and have an answer for the sin that comes can never be the Way for the Christian. Then, the value of these things depends on our doing them. But the doing is just our difficulty. We find we cannot do them, at least not as our conscience tells us they ought to be done. And because we fail to do them, they fail to bring us into the peace we need. Or if we think we have done them as they should be done, then they undo all the good they might have brought us by begetting in us the terrible sin of pride.

Not only, however, do they not bring us into peace, but the seeking of spiritual life by works can be positively harmful in another way. The unattained standards and the unfulfilled duties burden and condemn the conscience, and we sigh and drag our steps under the load. Paul was alluding to just this experience when he said, "The commandment, which was ordained to life (if I could keep it), I found to be unto death (because I failed to keep it)" (Rom. 7 : 10). The man who says,

"I believe in prayer", or "I believe in witnessing", or in any-thing else, will invariably end by being cursed by the very things in which he professes to have such faith, because sooner or later he is bound to fall down on those very things. Then his unattained standards will only nag him and he will be in bondage to them. As many as are of the works of the law are always under a curse, for according to moral law, cursed is every man who continues not in all the things, in which he professes to believe, to do them (Gal. 3 : 10). The only One we can believe in without being cursed is Jesus, because He has come to redeem us from the curse of our unattained standards, having been "made a curse for us" on Calvary (Gal. 3 : 13).

Only the Lord Jesus Himself is the Way; to attempt to walk on any other is to fall and to despair. This does not mean that we are not to do these things; of course they are to occupy a prominent place in the Christian's life. But it does mean to say that they are not the Way, as so often we make them. The Lord Jesus Himself is the Way. None else will suit our stumbling feet.

Someone at this point may object that he does not regard these things as the Way itself, but only as a way to Christ who is the true Way. *There is, however, no way to Christ, for Christ Himself is the Way.* We do not need a way to the Way. It is that little way to the Way that defeats us, and makes the real Way of none effect to us, because we cannot get there. In the early days of railways in Britain, some towns refused to have the railways go through them, because they feared that the sparks from the engine would set their property alight. Instead, the station was set on the outskirts of the town, to the immense inconvenience of later generations of townsmen. Not so this Way, which is Christ, for it runs right by us in our need and poverty, and we can find Him as we are and where we are. To say otherwise is to rob the Gospel of its sweetness.

We cannot but ask at this point, where do the means of grace come in; what is their proper place? Here we could not do better than quote from a recent writing * of the Rev.

* *Captivated by Christ*. Published by Christian Literature Crusade, U.S.A.

Wesley Nelson, of Oakland, California, both as making this point clear and as summarising much that has been already said:

"Because prayer is revitalised through fellowship with Christ, there is a tendency to look upon prayer as a way to Christ, and to try vainly to pray more fervently in order to come closer to Him. The Bible witnesses to Christ, and when Christ is near, the Bible is a new book. Therefore some torment themselves for not reading or studying it more faithfully in order to know Him better. Christ is the Way to the Bible, as He is to prayer. The Spirit of Christ Himself must speak through the pages of the Scriptures before they can become meaningful. The time of daily personal devotions becomes a more blessed experience to those who know Christ intimately. Sometimes this tends to be looked upon as a way to Christ, and the responsibility to keep it only adds to the burden of a troubled conscience. The sheep do not come to the still waters to find the Shepherd. It is the Shepherd Himself who leads them beside the still waters. Christ is immediately available right where we are, as we are. He in turn becomes the way to these various means of worship. He leads us into those forms of personal devotion and worship which are most adapted to each one's spiritual needs."

If, however, we have not a continuing devotional life with the Lord, expressing itself in prayer and feeding on His Word, it is because we have become spiritually cold and have got out of touch with the Lord. This is, perhaps, the surest index of where we are spiritually at any given time. In such a case the remedy is not, as is popularly supposed, to make a new attempt to pray and read the Bible more regularly, but to go direct to the Lord Jesus Himself to repent of the coldness and of the things that have caused it, and to receive from Him again His cleansing. Then it is that prayer and the study of His Word are suffused once more with the glory of His Presence and become a delight; and our witness to others becomes fresh and spontaneous. It is as simple as that! In this way we find Jesus to be the Way to our devotions, rather than our devotions the Way to Him—except in so far that in getting right with Him we do actually pray, and in dealing with us God invariably uses His Word.

* * * * *

Let us look now more positively at Jesus as the Way. Apart from Him, the sinner is faced with an excluding wall and the saint with impassable swamps. Both wall and swamps symbolise the same thing, sin. If it is sin that blocks the sinner's entrance, it is sin that impedes the saint's progress. With sin around him in the world, and sin within him in his heart, how can he hope to walk in fellowship with God? If the sinner needs a Door, the saint needs a Way—a Highway cast up, a Way prepared, along which he can walk in rest, joy, and power, through (or rather, above) the swamps of sin. As we have seen, Jesus Christ is that Way of rest, joy, and power, even as He was the Door of entrance.

The important thing, however, is to see that the very thing that made Him the Door makes Him the Way, too. It was not His life nor His teaching that made the Lord Jesus the Door, but rather His Cross, His blood, His finished work for sin. It is the same blood and finished work that constitutes Him the Way for us. It is redemption at the beginning of the Christian life and redemption all the way along. This means that this is a Way on which sin is anticipated, taken account of, and finished, even before it has come to existence in us. The worst discoveries we may make about ourselves do not take Him by surprise. The answer to sin is always there; indeed, the Way Himself is the answer. Here the convicted saint need not despair nor feel nagged, for his sin is cleansed and fellowship with God made real the moment it is confessed. Indeed, he need not regard himself as having slipped off the Way through his many sins of ignorance, if he gives an immediate and honest assent as soon as God shows them to him.

We may therefore call this Way the *Way of the Blood*. Indeed, in Hebrews 10 the new and living Way into the Holy of Holies of God's presence is clearly stated to be the blood of

Jesus (Heb. 10 : 19–22). Therefore, even the most self-condemned are bidden to have boldness to draw near by this Way, for it is consecrated for just such. Isaiah, too, prophesies the same comfort of this Way, as we have seen, when he speaks of "the Way of Holiness; the unclean shall not pass over it . . . but the redeemed shall walk there" (Isa. 35 : 8, 9). True, its title, the Way of Holiness, may at first sound forbidding, and the phrase, "the unclean shall not pass over it", may seem to exclude us. But who does walk there? It does not say "those who have never been unclean", or even "those who have only seldom been unclean", but "the redeemed", that is, those who on many or few occasions have been defiled by sin, but who have been redeemed by the blood of Christ, and who are continually cleansed just as often as may be necessary. This gives people no better than ourselves the chance to walk in daily, hourly fellowship with God, and takes from our souls all striving and strain as we do so, for "if we walk in the light, as He is in the light . . . the blood of Jesus Christ His Son cleanseth us from all sin" (1 John 1 : 7).

This Way is not only the Way of the blood, but also the *Way of Repentance*. If that which makes Jesus the Door—His blood—also makes Him the Way, then the steps of repentance and faith by which we entered through the Door are the constantly reiterated steps by which we walk the Way. There are not two messages, one for the unsaved and the other for the saved. It is the same blessed Lord who is presented to both, and the response which is required from both is that of repentance. It must ever be so when we speak of the blood of Jesus. If His blood, on the one hand, declares that sin is finished for us, it also demands, on the other hand, that sin should be admitted by us, for His blood only cleanses sin confessed as sin. When the Lord Jesus said, "I am the Way", He added, "and the Truth and the Life." Those two words do not introduce two entirely new thoughts, but refer back to "the Way" and qualify it. It was as if He were saying, "I am the Way, which is the Way of Truth and the Way of Life." This means that the light of Truth is always shining on this Highway, continually showing us the truth about ourselves and our sin. The thoughts and reactions of our hearts, the words of our lips, and the deeds of our hands are all spotlighted as sin by the light of Truth, whenever they are so, and we are required to agree continually with God under this conviction, and repent. This is what John calls "walking in the light, as He is in the light". If we are willing to say "Yes" to God under His light, then "we have fellowship one with another, and the blood of Jesus Christ His Son cleanses us from all sin". If, however, we refuse to say "Yes", and repent, then the walk with Jesus stops, we slip off the Highway, and we find ourselves in the darkness, where we are so much less able to see sin the next time. Very soon, if we still refuse, we shall be struggling again in the swamps. Thank God, we can always return to the Way the moment we are willing. The simple steps of repentance and faith in the blood of the Lord Jesus, by which we first entered the Door, have only to be repeated, and we are back with Him in the light. "If we confess our sins, He is faithful and just to forgive us our sins, and to cleanse us from all unrighteousness" (1 John 1 : 9).

This is what is meant by Isaiah's phrase, the Way of Holiness. It is what we may call Gospel holiness, the chief element of which is not that sin never comes, but that it is hated and judged and confessed to Jesus immediately it does come. Then, according to 1 Corinthians 1 : 30, He "is made unto us sanctification (that is, holiness)". He becomes to us what we cannot be in ourselves. We find ourselves possessed with a power that is not ours, and a holiness that is not ours either—but all His, who lives in us. So it is that victory ever comes by repentance —coupled with a simple trusting Him to be to us what He promises. The glorious fact is that we need not be defeated for any longer than it takes us to recognise sin as sin, and bring it to the Lord Jesus in confession. Then He not only cleanses and delivers but also becomes Himself our victory on that point, as we trust Him. What is this but continuous revival? The Way of Truth is found to be the Way of Life.

Most important, this Way is *simply walking with Jesus Himself.* The central phrase of Isaiah's prophecy of the Highway is, "He shall be with them" (Isa. 35 : 8 margin). He is both the Way itself and the One who walks beside us on that Way, bearing on His shoulders the responsibility of all our affairs. We can go shopping with Jesus, go to work with Him, do the most menial tasks in the house with Him, and undertake the largest responsibilities in our profession with Him. If we are cleansed from our sin as we go, we shall many times a day turn to Him to seek His guidance, to ask His help, or just to praise Him for His love and sufficiency. In no part of life are we to be independent of Him. His presence is to suffuse everything we do with peace. If in anything that peace is disturbed or shattered, we know that sin has come in, and we must repent, for the peace that comes from an ungrieved Holy Spirit in our hearts is the arbitrator over all that we do or think (Col. 3 : 15).

*   *   *   *   *

Before leaving this picture of the Lord Jesus as the Way, we need to point out its relevance to a matter which is rightly on the hearts of an increasing number of the Lord's people—the matter of the Church's need for revival.

It is not uncommon to hear of how the Holy Spirit has visited a Mission Station, a Bible School, or a Church in convicting power. Many Christians have been convicted of sin and broken before the Lord in repentance, and others have been saved for the first time. Hearts have been cleansed in the blood of Christ and filled with the Holy Spirit. Great joy has been in that place and the fruits of the Spirit have begun to appear in lives. After the disturbance of such an experience, sometimes involving the cessation for the time being of the usual routine, normal activities are resumed, albeit at a higher level. However, nobody seems to expect such times of humbling and cleansing to continue, and alas, they do not. Gradually the new life begins to recede, and the higher level at which all seemed to be living seems to drop, until not long after that time of outstanding blessing things are not much different from what they were before. And though perhaps not all the gains are lost, they are none the less left with little more than a bright memory which contrasts painfully with the present state of things. And what is true of the experience of a group is often true of the individual, who has to lament, "Where is the blessedness I knew?"

Now what has gone wrong here? In that time of revival we were in a crisis experience, a Door experience. The Spirit was convicting us, and we saw Jesus as the One who would bring us into peace and victory if we would repent. But we did not see that the steps of consenting to conviction, brokenness, and repentance which we were taking, were not only the Door but also the Way which we were to travel ever after. We certainly saw that those humbling steps were necessary to bring us into the state of peace and fellowship with God which we needed, but we did not expect to have to repeat them too often! Surely, we thought, the blessing we were entering into would last a more or less extended period! That was just the mistake we made. Those humbling steps needed to be often repeated; those steps should have become the habit of our soul. The crisis should have led us on to a walk, and a walk consists of reiterated steps, the same steps which we took in the crisis. As we have seen, the Lord Jesus is the Way as well as the Door, and the steps by which we entered are to be continually reiterated if we are to walk the way of peace, power, and rest. "As ye have therefore received Christ Jesus the Lord, so walk ye in Him" (Col. 2 : 6) continually. If we are to know His presence and power, there will have to be on our part continual willingness for conviction, a continual brokenness before the Lord, a continual repentance and a continual cleansing from sin in His blood, for sin makes its approach to us constantly. There is no such thing as a static experience of peace and holiness. Revival, holiness, and victory mean a constant walking with the Lord Jesus.

We once asked a missionary from one of the fields in East Africa where revival has been continuing for so many years, what was the leading feature, as he observed it, in the life of the fellowship out there. Without a moment's hesitation, he replied, "Living with Jesus in the Now." They were finding the Lord Jesus as the Way indeed.

And now a word as to recapturing the lost experience. An outstanding experience of being filled with the Spirit can sometimes prove more of a curse to us than a blessing, for if such an experience be lost, the devil uses the memory of it to nag us and condemn us. That which was ordained to be unto life we find to be unto death. More than that, the devil uses that past experience to provoke us to try to regain it by the way of works, and we get more and more into darkness and despair as our resolutions to do this or that prove abortive. The way back, however, is simple, so simple that it may elude us. It is simply to take our eyes off the blessings that Jesus gives, to cease to strive to recapture them, and to put our eyes on Jesus Himself, just as we are and where we are. Then He Himself will show us what is wrong with our present relationship with Him, and as we bow the head in repentance, we find Him again, but this time in a capacity more precious than ever before; as our new and living Way, involving us in a daily walk with Him in repentance and faith.

This Way may be thought of, then, variously as the Way of the Blood, or the Way of Repentance, or Walking with Jesus, or under some other term. They all mean the same. Christ Himself is the Way, and thereon His redemption is continually experienced. It is the primitive Way of the early Church which has today been lost sight of in the maze of merely human efforts and teachings, and has largely been superseded by the Way of works in its various subtle forms. As Jeremiah says, we have been caused to stumble in our ways from the ancient paths, to walk in bypaths, in a way not cast up (Jer. 18 : 15), in which there is little repentance and little of the joy of the redeemed. We need to rediscover each for himself that ancient path "where is the good way, and walk therein and ye shall find rest for your souls" (Jer. 6 : 16).

CHAPTER VIII

SEEING JESUS AS THE END

Now that we have seen the Way of the Blood of Jesus, and our need to walk it in repentance and true brokenness, we must ask ourselves, Where does it lead? What is its end? This is an important question, because the various ends we naturally set before ourselves in the Christian life are often very different from the one great End to this Way which God has appointed. It is this fact which accounts for the continual frustration we so often experience in our Christian lives and service.

The natural thing is for us to think that the way of repentance, humbling, and surrender will lead us to being made powerful in His service, to being much used of God in winning souls, to having our Church filled with an increasing number of seeking souls; in short, that it will lead to revival and to spiritual success. Much that we have read of the lives of outstanding men of God has led us to believe this. We have read that there came a time in their experience of being broken down before God, of full surrender, and of being filled with His Spirit, from which time it seemed God was able to use them mightily. How easy it is for us to think that if we go the same way we shall arrive at the same end. Even as we submit to the Spirit's conviction and seek to repent and surrender more completely, we have this end in mind, and there lurk mental pictures of what we shall become one day. I remember the embarrassment in my mind when, having given my testimony of the Lord's dealings with me to a fellow worker in the field of evangelism, he asked me, "Has all this meant more fruit in your meetings, more souls saved?" I was embarrassed because I could not say it had, and I felt it should have and I certainly wanted it to be so. It was the end expected both by myself and others, and I was disturbed that it had not worked out.

Others of us may be willing to let God deal with us, and to put things right, because we feel that in this way we are going to have peace and happiness and become the joyous, released personalities we have always longed to be. That is the end we have in mind. Yet others have the thought that if they are willing to be broken and repent, it will provoke the other person to repent too, and there will be a much-needed relief from tension in the home. That is the end in mind as they seek to respond to the Lord—an easier situation in the home. And so we could go on. None of us need look any farther than our own hearts to know the ends to which a full response to Christ is normally thought to lead, and which often become the motive for such a response. It is because these and similar things are ends that God seldom allows us to achieve them, and that we are characterised by so much striving and frustration. They are the wrong ends.

That this is so is made clear when we understand what Jesus said was the true End of the Way. To get His word on this point, we must go to John 14, the passage with which we have already been dealing, and in which He says, "I am the Way." Follow the argument of the passage. Jesus had said a surprising thing to His disciples, "Whither I go ye know, and the way ye know." Thomas replied (colloquialising it a little), "That is just what we don't know. We don't know whither, nor do we know the way." "Oh yes, you do know the Way," said the Lord in effect, "for I am the Way. Knowing Me, you know the Way." But where did the Way lead? To the Father, of course, for He went on, "No man cometh unto the Father but by Me." But the Father was not unknown to them either, for He continued, "If ye had known Me, ye should have known My Father also." Philip, quite puzzled, joined in at this point and said, "Lord, show us the Father and it sufficeth us." It was in reply to this that the Lord uttered the stupendous words, "He that hath seen Me hath seen the Father." Thus it was they discovered that they knew both the Way and the Whither, for the Lord Jesus was both. For us, too, He is both the Way and the Whither. In finding Him, men have not only found the Way, but the End, too. We do not have to go beyond Him to something else to satisfy our needs. He is the End of all that we need, and the simple, easily accessible Way to that End.

In the light of this we can see what some of us have been doing. *We have been availing ourselves of Jesus and His blood as the way, but to ends other than Himself.* We have been willing to go to all lengths to put things right, sometimes at great cost to ourselves, because the end we seek is seen to be so desirable. The intensely earnest soul will pray, "God, I will pay any cost to have revival, to enjoy Thy power on my ministry." But in the shadows around those ends there often lurk the subtle motives of self-interest and self-glory. Little wonder, then, that in spite of our agonisings in prayer, God has not allowed us to reach those ends. Even if our motives are quite free from self-interest, those things are still not to be the end nor the reason for which we get right with the Lord. Our end is to be the Lord Jesus Himself. The reason for which we are to get right, is not that we might have revival, or power, or to be used of God, or have this or that blessing, *but that we might have Him.* Our sin has caused us to slip His hand; a cloud has come between His lovely face and ourselves, and at all costs we want to find Him and His fellowship again. That, and that only, is to be the reason why we should be willing to go the way of repentance—not for any other motive than that we want Him. He is to be the End; but alas, other ends, idols all of them, have taken His place in our hearts.

The story of the ten leprous men who were healed by the Lord Jesus is a graphic illustration of this. Of the ten, only one, when he discovered himself healed, returned to Jesus to give Him thanks and glorify God. The other nine held on their way, eager to enjoy the new life into which their healing from leprosy had introduced them. To them the Lord Jesus was but the means to the end, the end being a life of health. But to the other who fell down at His feet, craving fellowship with the One who had healed him, He was not only the means but the End Himself.

Such is the humility of our adorable Lord that He is willing in the first days of our spiritual experience to be a means to such ends as peace and happiness and power. Indeed, with men in their sins, enlightened self-interest is all that God has to appeal to. What is the Gospel appeal—"Flee from the wrath to come"—but an appeal to such self-interest? And, as I say, He is willing for us to see Him and His atoning Cross a Way to such an escape, such an end. But not for long can He allow us to go on making Him the means to ends other than Himself. He knows all such ends will not satisfy our hearts, for we are made for Him, and we are restless till we rest in Him. Moreover, such ends, if that is all we come to, would fail to satisfy His heart, for the Bible tells us that the whole purpose of Jesus on the Cross was to reconcile us *"unto Him-self"* (2 Cor. 5 : 19). Again, we are told that God has "pre-destinated us unto the adoption of children by Jesus Christ *to Himself"* (Eph. 1 : 5), and that Jesus gave Himself for us "that He might . . . purify *unto Himself* a peculiar people" (Titus 2 : 14)

So it is that He allows us to be frustrated and disappointed in our strivings after this or that end until at last He comes to us and says, "My child, I never promised you that if you would surrender, repent and get right with Me, you would have an eased situation, great power, success in your service, or even revival. What I do promise you is that, if you will walk with Me, and allow Me to show you sin as soon as it comes in and cleanse you from it, you will have not these things, but—Me. Make Me your End and you will surely have that End, and you shall be satisfied, lacking nothing that is in the will of God for you." The shameful thing is, however, that, when this comes home to us, we feel a little disappointed. We have to admit it was not Himself we really wanted, but rather His gifts, and that for subtle, selfish reasons! As the hymn writer says, "I yearned for them, not Thee." That is why He has not allowed us to have them!

This explains to me something that used to puzzle me in my early Christian service. Years ago, in my evangelistic ministry, it appeared to me that the key to the situation was the Christians. If there was a blockage of sin there, then the Holy Spirit could not work amongst the unconverted. I could find,

I thought, various Scriptures to support this view. It seemed
clear that if the Christians would repent of their sins and get
right with God, then the Holy Spirit would be free to move in
power amongst the lost. Consequently, I began to devote the
first week of my campaigns to speaking to Christians and calling them to repentance, and very often God blessed them
greatly, and there was real repentance at the Cross. But when,
in the second week, we turned especially to the unconverted,
things were sometimes difficult, and there was not always the
mighty working of God that I thought there should have been.
The reason now is clear. Our repenting and getting right with
God was a means to an end, the end being that souls should
be saved—an end other than Jesus Himself. We had our eye
on that all the time we were getting right, and that was why
God could not set His seal to it. We were repenting "under
law" as a sort of bargain with God. We were ultimately driven
to God in prayer, and when at last souls were saved, it was not
because we had repented, but because He was gracious. We
should have got right just because we were wrong and because
we loved Jesus, and our sins had made Him hide His lovely
face from us, and at all costs we wanted Him back. That such
revived, radiant Christians would be a powerful inducement
to the lost to turn to Christ is indeed a fact, but that would not
be the end for which they repented.

The wonderful thing is, however, that when we are willing
to be convicted of the sin of making these other things our
ends, and to have the Lord Jesus as our only end, God delights
to give us with Him many of these very things which we are
now not seeking first. "How shall He not with Him also freely
give us all things?" (Rom. 8 : 32). And who can tell what is
not included of His generosity in those "all things"? What
wonderful things will He not do for those who are willing to
walk with the Lord Jesus for His own sake!

Perhaps the best illustration of this is the incident of
Solomon asking for wisdom (1 Kings 3 : 5–13) When God said
to Solomon: "Ask what I shall give thee", he was, so to speak,
offered a blank cheque. Instead of seeking selfish ends, he
simply asked: "Give therefore Thy servant an understanding

heart to judge Thy people." The margin puts it—"a hearing heart", that is, a disposition of brokenness which is willing to listen to God, and to be told what to do. God was so delighted that Solomon made this the end that he was seeking that He said: "Because thou hast asked this thing, and hast not asked for thyself long life; neither hast asked riches for thyself, nor hast asked the life of thine enemies, but hast asked for thyself understanding to discern judgment; behold, I have done according to thy words: lo, I have given thee a wise and an understanding heart." He got the end that he was seeking. But that was not all: "I have also given thee that which thou hast not asked, both riches, and honour: so that there shall not be any among the kings like unto thee all thy days." God threw in with the one thing he desired the many other things which had ceased to be chief ends for him, and God did so just because they had ceased to be such to him. So it will be with us when we, too, cease to make other selfish things the end, and are content to see in Jesus only our end. With Him God will give us all that is in His will for us.

*   *   *   *   *

We have just considered the ends which we seek, which come *short of Christ*. Sometimes, however, we find ourselves seeking ends *beyond Him*.

We may not fail to see the importance of the way of repentance, and the need for the cleansing of the blood of Christ. We may be those who are open to the conviction of the Holy Spirit, and are willing to come back to the Cross when necessary. But we feel that the blessing we seek, and need so much, still lies beyond. This applies very much to our search for such blessings as victory, power, healing, the fulness of the Spirit, and even revival itself. We believe the blood of Christ and our repentance certainly provide the way to that blessing, but not the very blessing itself. We are convinced that to get right with God at the Cross is but the preparation for God's mighty moving in on us. For that we still have to pray and struggle and wait, we feel. We think we must now go on from Calvary to some other place in experience, say, Pentecost, and that the place of repentance at Jesus' feet must be left for some much more positive position.

Reasonable as all this may sound, the result is invariably the same—we have not found the End which we seek. We are left still searching and dissatisfied, still without the glowing testimony, "I have found."

Surely God has something better for us than this. He has indeed, but only by our seeing His Son as the End as well as the Way. If the Lord Jesus said that in coming to Him men have found not only the Way to the Father, but the Father Himself, surely He means that to apply to every other blessing we seek. The glorious truth is that He is Himself not only the Way to blessing, but the needed blessing itself; not only the Way to power, but our power; not only the Way to victory, but our victory; not only the Way to sanctification, but our sanctification; not only the Way to healing, but our healing; not only the Way to revival, but our revival, and so on for everything else. He is Himself made to us what we need. In Him dwells all the fulness of the Godhead bodily, as Paul says, and we are complete in Him (Col. 2 : 10). In coming to Him as a sinner, as so often we must, we find Him to be *just there* all we need. We do not have to go any farther than the Cross into a blessing, which we imagine lies beyond. Pentecost is found, not at Pentecost, but at Calvary, where sinners repent, as is also revival and every other blessing. Way and End are the One Person, found together in the one moment of each successive act of repentance and faith.

We are now in a position to understand the reasons for many of the frustrations in the spiritual life. We have sought peace, holiness, victory, revival as blessings apart from and additional to the Lord Jesus, and they have for this reason eluded us. We have prayed and struggled for them and sought to fulfil all sorts of conditions, but in vain. We have even been willing to walk the humbling Way of the blood of Jesus, and to let Him convict us and bring us to repentance; but even so the great baptism of love and power is looked upon as something yet to be received.

In contrast to this, let us ponder again Paul's great word,

"Christ is the end of the law for righteousness to every one that believeth" (Rom. 10 : 4). J. B. Phillips, in his well-known colloquial translation of the epistles, quotes it, "Christ is the end of the struggle for righteousness-by-the-law to everyone that believes." * What a pregnant phrase, Christ is the end of the struggle! That for which earnest Jews struggled in those days was righteousness. This is not, in the first place, personal righteousness of character, but something even greater than that—being right with God, or what we may call rightness with God. In going through the Epistle to the Romans, it is helpful whenever you come to the word "righteousness" to read "rightness with God", for that gives the meaning of the word as Paul uses it. It was to achieve this rightness with God that the Jew struggled to keep his complicated law, but his failure to do so only condemned him in his heart, and the assurance that he was right with God on that ground seemed the more removed the more he tried. It was into this state of need that the apostle came with his glorious message, "Christ is the end of the struggle for rightness with God to every one that believes." Christ had borne on the Cross for them the curse of the Divine law which they had so often broken, and now His blood was reckoned to them as their perfect rightness with God even while they were still sinners, provided they repented and put their faith in Christ. What was before to them but the distant end of many struggles was the beginning and basis of a new life received from Christ, from which they could go on. They were given the privilege of beginning at the end!

The Lord Jesus, however, is not only the end of our struggles for rightness with God, but for everything else—for peace, for victory, for holiness, for healing, for revival. What struggles we have had to obtain these blessings, what excruciating surrenders sometimes, what prayings, what self-mortifications, what battles to make our sinful hearts less sinful. But in coming to Him in helpless repentance and confession of sin we have come to the One who in the moment of our abasement is the very blessing we have been struggling for in so many

* J. B. Phillips in *Letters to Young Churches*

other directions. He is our peace; He is our power; He is our victory; He is our revival. There is nothing beyond Him.

> The well is deep and I require
>   A draught of the Water of Life;
> And none can meet my soul's desire
>   For a draught of the Water of Life;
> Till One draws near who the cry will heed,
>   Helper of men in their time of need,
> And I, believing, find indeed
>   That *Christ is the Water of Life.*

How often, however, is it otherwise with earnest Christians? I shall never forget sharing in a Conference in Alsace some few years ago, and having the privilege of working with an African leader, deeply taught of the Lord and possessed of that rare gift, the gift of revival leadership. The Lord had worked deeply, many had been convicted and melted, and, having come to the Lord Jesus with all that He had shown them, were gloriously set free and were returning home with their "cups running over" with praise to God. A small group who had been at the Conference, and who had been blessed like so many others, approached us and asked us if we would speak the next day at their prayer meeting for revival in the town near by. They told us that they had been meeting two or three times a week for several years, praying for revival, and now of course they were going to pray more than ever for revival. It was only before the meeting that the situation really dawned on us. Here were a people who had seen Jesus anew, had been convicted of their sins and knelt at His feet, and were freshly filled with Himself—and they were going to go on praying for revival! This meant that they had seen Jesus only as the way to revival, and not as Revival itself. God gently showed them through the lips of that African leader that they were doing what many of the people did in the days when our Lord Jesus first appeared on the scene in Judea. They were still waiting for and praying for the coming of their Messiah, when all the time He stood there among them, unknown and unrecognised. Maybe He did not fulfil at that time their mental picture of what Messiah would be, but today He is at the right hand of the Majesty on High, Messiah indeed. In the same way, what

God does in our hearts in the way of convicting and melting may not fulfil the traditional conception of revival; but if Jesus has come afresh into the central place, be assured it is revival; and who knows where this will end if we go on walking with Him?

It may be asked, Are we not, then, to pray for revival? Our first responsibility is to be revived ourselves, and to have a testimony that we have come to the end of our struggle and that we have found Jesus Himself as all we need, with all that that involves of repentance. Then we, and others in fellowship can pray that what God has done in our hearts He will do in other hearts in ever-widening circles. We are not, then, praying for revival as something that has not yet come, but as Someone who has already come to our hearts, if to none others as yet. Revival has begun (and it has begun, even if the Reviver has come to only one heart), and it is now but a matter of it spreading. The beach-head for new life established in but a few hearts needs now to be extended to other hearts, and to that end God will use our testimony and willingness for self-giving quite as much as our prayers. Such prayers, however, will be offered by those who know they have found both the Way and the End; the striving and tenseness that characterise so much of our praying for revival will be absent, and a calm confidence and boldness will take their place.

Does all this mean that the one who has found both the Way and the End in the Lord Jesus has attained all the heights of spirituality that God has for him? By no means! He is still a sinner; he still needs the blood of Jesus; he still repents. Indeed, he is quicker to repent than ever, for part of his discovery is that the way of repentance is the way of proving the Lord Jesus as his all. What, then, has such a man found? He has found at last where the true gold is, and has sunk his shaft into that precious vein, the Lord Jesus. He is not now shaken or disturbed by the report of "lucky strikes" anywhere else, in this doctrine, or that experience, or the other emphasis. And the strange thing is, that after all his attempts to find the answer in so many other directions, he has come back to the very same shaft he sank when God first saved him, that which

CHAPTER IX

SEEING JESUS—FOR OTHERS

IT is only when we have truly seen the Lord Jesus to be the End that we have come to the beginning of the real Christian life that God has for us. As we have seen, what previously was the far-distant End—righteousness, peace with God, holiness, revival—to be achieved only after many struggles, now becomes the beginning for us. We have found Christ Himself to be for us all those things, and we have seen His precious blood to be the easily accessible way to that End. We are now given the privilege of beginning at the End!

Now, what is involved in this new beginning? We hardly need to ask the question, for instinctively everyone who makes this new discovery knows that it is for others. The new testimony which such a one gives is not only that his Lord might be glorified, but that others should share the same life that he is enjoying. Indeed, it is the spreading of this new life in Christ to others which is the spreading of revival.

Those whose normal climate of living is that of law rather than of grace will feel they are at last on familiar ground, and will expect here at least some exhortation as to what they have to do in the way of witnessing, soul-winning, reaching others, etc. But no, not even here does grace quit the field. There never comes a time when grace ends and self has to begin again, and this applies to what we call our service as much as to any other part of our Christian lives. In no place do we need to know the Way of Grace more than in the impartation of this Life to others. Our service for our fellows does not come from strained efforts on our part to live for them, but rather from seeing Jesus doing so, and then simply making ourselves available to Him that we may be the channel of His grace and power to them. This was the way in which He walked in His relationship with the Father, and it is the way in which we must walk in our relationship with Him. Said He, "The Son can do nothing of Himself, but what He seeth the Father do: for what things soever He doeth, these also doeth the Son likewise" (John 5 : 19). And we, too, can do nothing but what we see the Lord Jesus doing. Until we see that, we are helpless, and our service is nothing more than self-initiated striving. But if we will first seek to see what the Lord Jesus is doing in a situation, then we can move with Him, even as the Son moved with the Father, and in that co-operation between man and God the true works of God are produced. Ours is not to originate anything, but simply to yield ourselves to Him to be the channel of what He initiates and carries through, and to trust Him to do so through us.

Let us state the truth simply and boldly—the Lord Jesus is for others. Just as the vine does not bear its grapes for its own refreshment but for the refreshment of others, so has this Divine Vine chosen to be and to act only and always for others. All He did was for others. When He came from heaven, it was for others. When He laid down His life, it was for others. Even when He was raised again from the dead, it was quite as much to justify others as to justify Himself and His claims (Rom. 4 : 24). Furthermore, the position He occupies just now in heaven is for others, for we read that He has entered "into heaven itself, now to appear in the presence of God for us" (Heb. 9 : 24). We sing about His present "riches in glory all His own", but whereas they are His own, He only holds them for us. The Father has raised up His Son and appointed Him to be all the time for others, others, others; and you and I are those guilty, undeserving others.

Not only is this what He is, but this determines what His purpose is. It is to recover these others to God and Himself through the redemption of His Cross, by the mighty working of His Holy Spirit among them. This is no wishful thinking on His part, but a settled Divine purpose which is backed by all the resources of heaven, and is therefore certain of fulfilment. And today, all over this world, redeemed at the cost of His blood, Jesus the Vine is bringing forth His fruit for the healing of the nations, and dying sinners, tasting of that fruit, live.

The Lord Jesus, however, is not alone in this. He draws redeemed men into co-operation with Himself in the outworking of His glorious purposes, and they become His branches on which His fruit is borne. Just as apart from Him the branches can do nothing of themselves, so it is that apart from them the Vine does not bear fruit. They do not, however, produce or initiate the fruit; that is altogether His work. They simply bear what He produces as He lives His life again in them.

This is exactly the picture that the Lord Jesus gives us in John 15 of our relationship with Himself when He says, "I am the Vine, ye are the branches." The believer is constituted a branch in Christ who comes to dwell in him.

> Just as the branch is to the vine,
> I'm joined to Christ; I know He's mine!

This means that he is made a part of the One who lives and acts only for the salvation and blessing of men, and He designs to bear His fruit for them on just such a branch. What a comfort to us, when conscious of our weakness, to know He is the Vine! But on the other hand, with what boldness and authority does not this endue us as we move among needy, hungry men—I am His branch, a part of Him whose resources are limitless for the blessing of these men around me!

*　　*　　*　　*　　*

Let us look more closely at this parable of the Vine and the branches, which illustrates more clearly than perhaps any other Scripture our union with the Lord Jesus.

He begins by saying, "I am the true Vine". The construction of the sentence in the Greek gives special emphasis to the word "true". Quite obviously the Lord is contrasting Himself with another vine that was not the true vine, which proved a failure. The Old Testament abounds in references to this vine. The Psalmist says, "Thou hast brought a vine out of Egypt: Thou hast cast out the heathen, and planted it. Thou preparest room before it, and didst cause it to take deep root, and it filled the land" (Psa. 80 : 8, 9). This vine was Israel, and God's intention in bringing them out of Egypt and planting them in their own land was that they might bring forth fruit for the nations, that in them all nations of the world should be blessed. But that vine failed of that high purpose, for they regarded their privileges and blessings as being only for themselves, and turned away from their God to idols. So it is we hear God saying, "Israel is an empty vine, he bringeth forth fruit unto himself" (Hos. 10 : 1). There was plenty of foliage, but no fruit for God or man. Again, He laments in another place concerning Israel, "I had planted thee a noble vine, wholly a right seed: how then art thou turned into the degenerate plant of a strange vine unto Me?" (Jer. 2 : 21).

The most dramatic passage, however, about the failure of this Old Testament vine is the beautiful song of the vineyard in Isaiah 5 :

"My wellbeloved hath a vineyard in a very fruitful hill; and he fenced it, and gathered out the stones thereof, and planted it with the choicest vine, and built a tower in the midst of it, and also made a winepress therein: and he looked that it should bring forth grapes, and it brought forth wild grapes. And now, O inhabitants of Jerusalem, and men of Judah, judge, I pray you, betwixt me and my vineyard. What could have been done more to my vineyard, that I have not done in it? wherefore, when I looked that it should bring forth grapes, brought it forth wild grapes?"

What a parable this is, not only of Israel, but of ourselves! What could have been done more to us that God has not done for us? Many of us can look back on a good and godly upbringing, when we were spared much that has spoilt other lives. Then came the day, when hearing the message of grace, we received Jesus Christ as our Saviour. Those days were followed by marvellous privileges and blessings denied many others. We were taught, perhaps, by teachers well versed in the Scriptures; we enjoyed the fellowship of other saints; a sphere of service lay ready at our hand, and God poured innumerable blessings into our laps. Nor did we lack the personal attention of the Vine-dresser, for He came to us often in pruning and in healing. Of each of us in varying degrees God has to say, "What could have been done more to My vineyard that I have not done in it?" And yet when He looked for grapes, the fruit of the Spirit, that would glorify Him and bless others, we brought forth only wild, bitter grapes, the ugly works of the flesh. Look again at these works which all too often are all that God has got from us. "The works of the flesh are manifest, which are these:

> Fornication,
> uncleanness,
> lasciviousness,
> idolatry,
> sorcery,
> enmities,
> strife,
> jealousies,
> wraths,
> factions,
> divisions,
> parties,
> envyings,
> drunkenness,
> revellings, and such like" (Gal. 5 : 19–21, R.V.).

There is everything here that is sour and hurtful, from sexual impurity to jealousy and a party spirit, but nothing for God or man. This is the fruit that we have served to those at home, at work, and even in our church. And all this has been produced on a vine on which God has lavished so many privileges and so much care. And, strange to say, this has been the state of things, even when we vowed that it should be otherwise, and struggled to make it so.

Now, why should this be our experience? Why was this the state of things with Israel, God's Old Testament vine? The simple reason was that Israel was the vine, and just as long as Israel was the vine, she could not but produce this kind of fruit, for such fruit is characteristic of fallen human nature, for its centre is ever itself. If human nature could have been improved to produce sweet grapes, then it would have been seen in Israel's case, for no vine received so much from God as they did. But in the failure of Israel was demonstrated the complete inability of man ever to be a vine to produce fruit for God. This, then, is the reason for our failure, too. It is simply that we have been trying to be the vine; we have been trying to find a holiness and a love for others in ourselves and from ourselves which Scripture never encourages us to expect to find there. We have discovered what Paul had to discover long before us, when he said, "I know that in me (that is, in my flesh), dwelleth no good thing" (Rom. 7 : 18). Another who made the same discovery once prayed, "O God, forgive me the wrong I do by being me."

This, then, was the vine with which the Lord Jesus contrasted Himself. Thus it was that, standing in the midst of the ruins of the vine which had been such a sorrow to God, He cried, "I am the true Vine." It was as if He said, "Man's day of being the vine is over. God's judgment of him as the vine is to be completed in My body on the Tree. From now on, I am the Vine. From Me now is God's fruit to be found and from nowhere else." Rightly understood this is the best news we could have. God no longer expects us to be the vine. We need not even try. The responsibility for producing fruit is no longer ours. God has His own true Vine, the risen Lord Jesus, who is well able to produce all the fruit that God requires for others, and to fulfil all the purposes of His grace for men.

But we—where do we come in? Simply as branches in Him, the Vine. We do not produce the fruit, but simply bear what He produces, as we permit Him to live in us. This throws a new light on those words of Paul, "I am crucified with Christ; nevertheless I live" (Gal. 2 : 20). There is a Paul here who was crucified with Christ, and a Paul who none the less lives. Which is which? The Paul who was crucified with Christ was Paul the vine, the man who vainly tried to do his best. The Paul who nevertheless lived was Paul, the branch, the man who was broken as to his self-confidence, and was dependent on his Lord. And in Paul, the branch, the Lord Jesus lived His life again, for he goes on to say immediately, "yet not I, but Christ liveth in me", just as the vine by its sap lives in the branch. Jesus became for Him the Vine, the source of all the fruitage that was seen in his life and service.

*   *   *   *   *

We come now to the practical implementing of all this in our daily experience.

It is possible for any of us at any time to assume the position, often unconsciously, of the vine. We start the day as if it were *our* day and we make *our* plans for *our* day and fully intend to do *our* best for the Lord. The responsibility and government is really on our shoulders, and we have subtly become the vine. But just because it is our day and we are the vine, things soon go wrong. People and circumstances upset our schedule and interfere with what we wanted to do, and there is a reaction of hardness, irritation, and resentment in our hearts, and often the sharp retort on our lips. The very responsibility of trying to be the vine makes us tense, and tenseness always predisposes us to further sin. If we are charged with the responsibility of some special piece of Christian service, our tenseness and reactions are often far worse, and we can go into that piece of service without calling them sin. It is little wonder that we return abashed and defeated.

The way of repentance, however, is ever open to us. Our true Vine, Jesus Himself, has, like many an ordinary vine, been tied to a stake, the stake of Calvary. He invites us to return to Him in repentance and to confess the source of these things as being our attempt to be ourselves the vine, receiving from His hands forgiveness and cleansing. Immediately He becomes the Vine to us again and we become the branch that rests in Him. And in the very place of failure, we have the fruits of the Spirit, the products of His life and nature. What an array of precious grapes they are, all of them for the blessing of others and all of them characteristic of Himself! What a contrast to the works of the flesh, so characteristic of us! "The fruit of the Spirit is:

> love,
> joy,
> peace,
> longsuffering,
> gentleness,
> goodness,
> faith,
> meekness,
> self-control" (Gal. 5 : 22, 23).

Inasmuch as the Scripture does not speak of the fruits of the Spirit, but rather of the fruit (in the singular) of the Spirit, it would seem that all of them are components of the first one mentioned, the all-inclusive fruit of love, His love for the other man.

The way of victory is, however, always by repentance. Jesus cannot be the Vine to us, except as we repent of the works of the flesh as God shows them to us. A mere attempt to trust Him more completely and to rest in Him, without an acknowledgment of the sin there is, never brings victory, His victory. He is only the Vine to me as I repent of trying to be the vine myself. It is only as I repent of my unlove that I have His love; only as I confess my worry and lack of peace that I have His peace; only as I confess my impatience that I have His long-suffering; only as I confess my resentment that I have His meekness, and so on.

More than that, when we are willing for Him to be the Vine and we but the branch, His purposes of salvation and blessing for other lives begin to be worked out. Things just happen, marvellous things. Being what He is, it could hardly be otherwise. Being a marvellous Lord, marvellous things are just normal to Him. He does not need us to persuade Him to save and revive others. This is His work. He does not begin to work only when we begin to pray and believe. He is working like this all the time, only we have not been linked to Him. But when we begin to pray, and (even more important than prayer) when we begin to believe, we are caught up into the purposes in which He is already engaged and become the branches on which His fruit is borne. The degree in which this is our experience is simply the degree in which we expect it of Him.

* * * * *

Finally, we now come to ask, What is our part as branches if His fruit is to be borne on us and His purposes fulfilled through us?

First, we must be continually seeing by faith Jesus to be the Vine, the One who is love for others and who is working out His purposes of grace towards them in the power of His limitless resources. He is never at a loss, never discouraged, never defeated, and He is our Vine! Our weakness and emptiness is no hindrance to Him; indeed, it gives Him the more room in which to prove Himself. What a sight of Him to fill our vision! Boldness, confidence, and assurance spring up in our hearts as the natural result. As we become victorious in spirit, the battle is won before it is begun, and His fruits cannot but appear.

Second, there must be the willingness to be broken and become available to Him as a branch. A branch has no independent life of its own. It exists only to bear the fruit of the Vine. So it must be with us in our relationship to the Lord Jesus. What a battle there is in our hearts so often with our selfishness and personal interests! So often we are just not available to Him because we have lapsed back to our old centre, self. But it must be surrendered if we are to be available to Him as His branch, and that not just in one sweeping surrender, which we may make in a solemn moment of dedication, but just as things come up and as He deals with us. This will involve a continuous dying to self and its rights and wishes, but only so can the Lord Jesus bring forth His fruit on the branch.

A word of testimony will illustrate this point. The writer was travelling by train to conduct some meetings. He had to change trains twice before he reached his destination. For the first part of the journey he was buried in his newspaper, and although he was conscious of a little Voice telling him he ought to have a heart for the others in the compartment, he was unwilling to lay aside his paper. He was not available to the Vine. On the second part of his journey, he was occupied in preparing his message for the meeting at which he was to preach. Once again the little Voice told him he should have a heart for the others around him. But he was tense and anxious about the meeting ahead of him, and he felt he must continue. Once again he was not available. But as he approached the third part of his journey, the Lord Jesus broke him and he at last told the Lord Jesus of his willingness to be His branch. The compartment into which he now entered was empty, and he wondered if God really had been speaking to him. Very soon a man came in, and continued to be the only occupant with him until the end of the journey. The conversation was easily turned to spiritual things and to the man's need of the Lord Jesus. He proved to be a prepared heart indeed. Five minutes from the destination he received Him as his personal Saviour there in the train, and letters from him have since evidenced the fact that God did a work in his heart that day. That very experience gave the writer the fresh vision of His Lord that he needed at that time, a new confidence in Him sprang up in his heart, and in the days that followed he saw the Lord Jesus bring revival and salvation to a church in a way in which he had seldom seen before.

This blessed Vine, then, is compassionate and touched with the needs of men, but we are selfish and unconcerned. This Vine exists just for others, but we are self-centred. This Vine is gloriously sufficient to implement His own purposes of love for men, but we are unbelieving and not available. May God deal with us and break us so that we shall be willing to be available to Him as His branches!

*　　*　　*　　*　　*

We are now in a position to consider the meaning of the word which the Lord Jesus used to describe our part in this life. Said He, "Abide in Me, and I in you" (John 15 : 4). It is well that we have kept this word to the very end, for it has often loomed too large in the thinking of earnest, seeking souls. It has often been said, "The secret is in the abiding." But that is not so, for it makes the secret to reside in something we do, and this can only lead to yet another form of striving, the striving to abide. The secret surely lies in the Vine, and the blessing comes from our seeing Him as such—and as we see Him, before we know it, we are abiding!

The word to "abide" simply means to "dwell" or "remain" or "continue". God has placed us in His Son, united us to Him as a branch is to the Vine. Let us simply remain there, dwell there, continue there, abide there, in Him. If we do this, then He on His part promises to dwell, remain, abide in us. "Abide in Me" is the condition which we are to fulfil. "I in you" is the promise which He will fulfil. It is as if He says, "If you will dwell in Me, I will dwell in you." And when He is living again His life in us, His fruit and victory cannot but be manifest, for He never fails.

In what, then, does abiding in Christ consist? The word must be interpreted in the light of all we have said of Jesus, the Vine. It consists, first, in a willingness to repent quickly whenever sin comes in, because we have assumed the position of the vine. This continually puts us in our right position as branches. Second, it means continually seeing Jesus as the Vine, living and acting for others in the power of His limitless resources. Then there is the continuous faith that reckons on its union with this precious Vine. Such faith does not ask to be united to Him, but takes its stand that it is united already, and praises Him for His life made ours. With that there is the brokenness that continually yields its rights and interests to Jesus, that it might be available to Him as His branch for blessing others. Lastly, there is the pouring out of love to others, not in word only but in deed. As we begin to pour out, He pours in of His love. But if we will not begin to pour out, He cannot pour in. It is only as we turn the tap, and begin to draw off water, that fresh water is poured into the tank. The latter is actually the only definition in John 15 that Jesus Himself gives of abiding, and therefore must include every other part. Said He, "If ye keep My commandments, ye shall